WORKINGTON
IRON AND STEEL

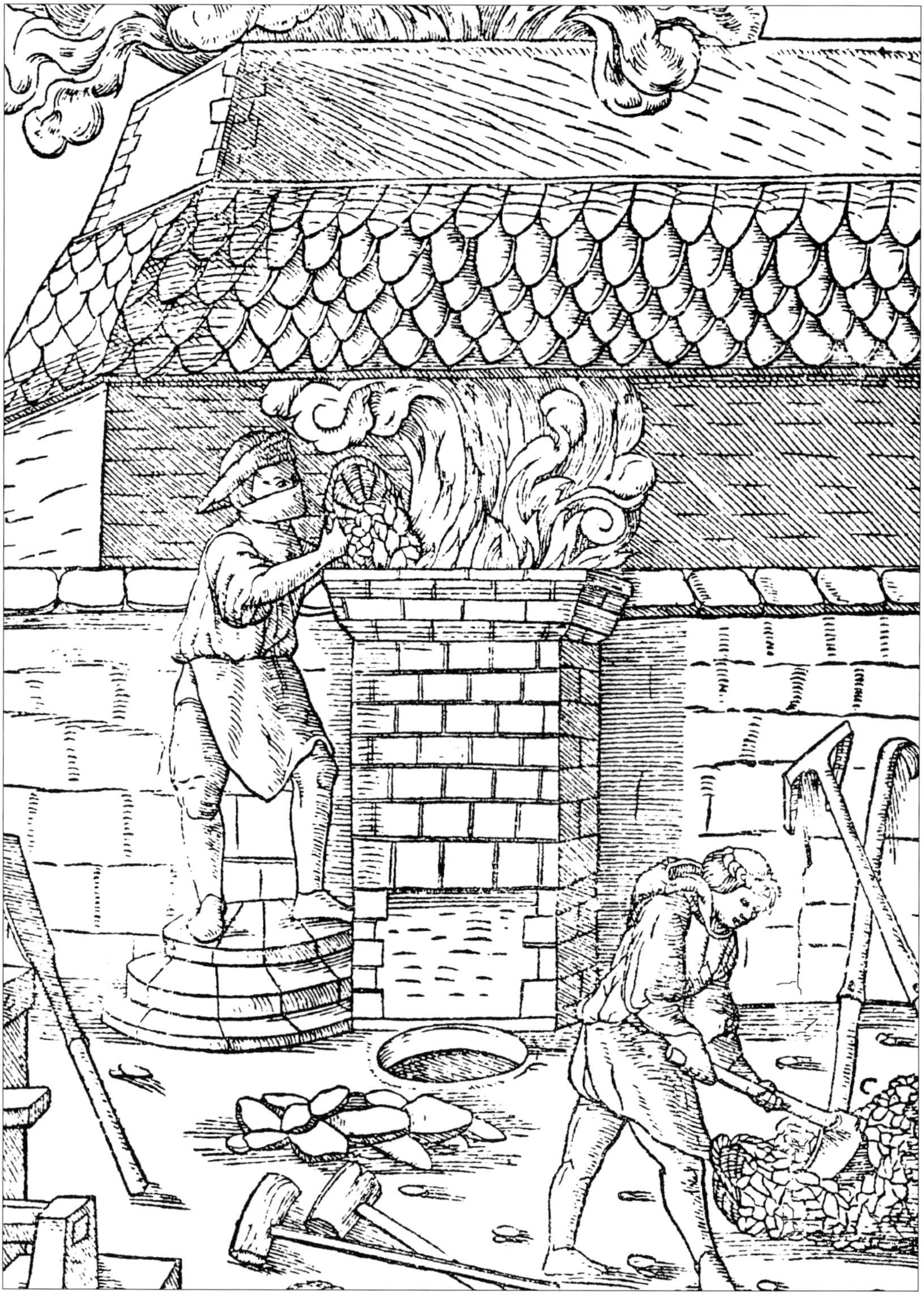

WORKINGTON

IRON AND STEEL

RICHARD L.M. BYERS

TEMPUS

First published 2004

Tempus Publishing Limited
The Mill, Brimscombe Port,
Stroud, Gloucestershire, GL5 2QG
www.tempus-publishing.com

© Richard L.M. Byers, 2004

The right of Richard L.M. Byers to be identified as the
Author of this work has been asserted in accordance with
the Copyrights, Designs and Patents Act 1988.

All rights reserved. No part of this book may be reprinted
or reproduced or utilised in any form or by any electronic,
mechanical or other means, now known or hereafter invented,
including photocopying and recording, or in any information
storage or retrieval system, without the permission in writing
from the Publishers.

British Library Cataloguing in Publication Data.
A catalogue record for this book is available from the British Library.

ISBN 0 7524 3196 X

Typesetting and origination by Tempus Publishing Limited.
Printed in Great Britain.

Contents

	Introduction	7
one	Barepot or Seaton Ironworks	9
two	Workington Haematite Iron Co. Workington Haematite Iron & Steel Co. Workington Iron Co. Oldside Iron & Steel Works	17
three	West Cumberland Haematite Iron Co. West Cumberland Iron & Steel Co. North Western Iron & Steel Co.	25
four	North of England Haematite Ironworks Lowther Haematite Iron Co. Lowther Haematite Iron & Steel Co.	33
five	Moss Bay Haematite Iron Co. Moss Bay Haematite Iron & Steel Co.	39
six	New Yard Ironworks	55
seven	Derwent Haematite Ironworks Charles Cammell & Co. Ltd Cammell Laird & Co. Ltd	61
eight	Workington Iron & Steel Co. United Steel Companies	69
	Bibliography	124
	Index	125

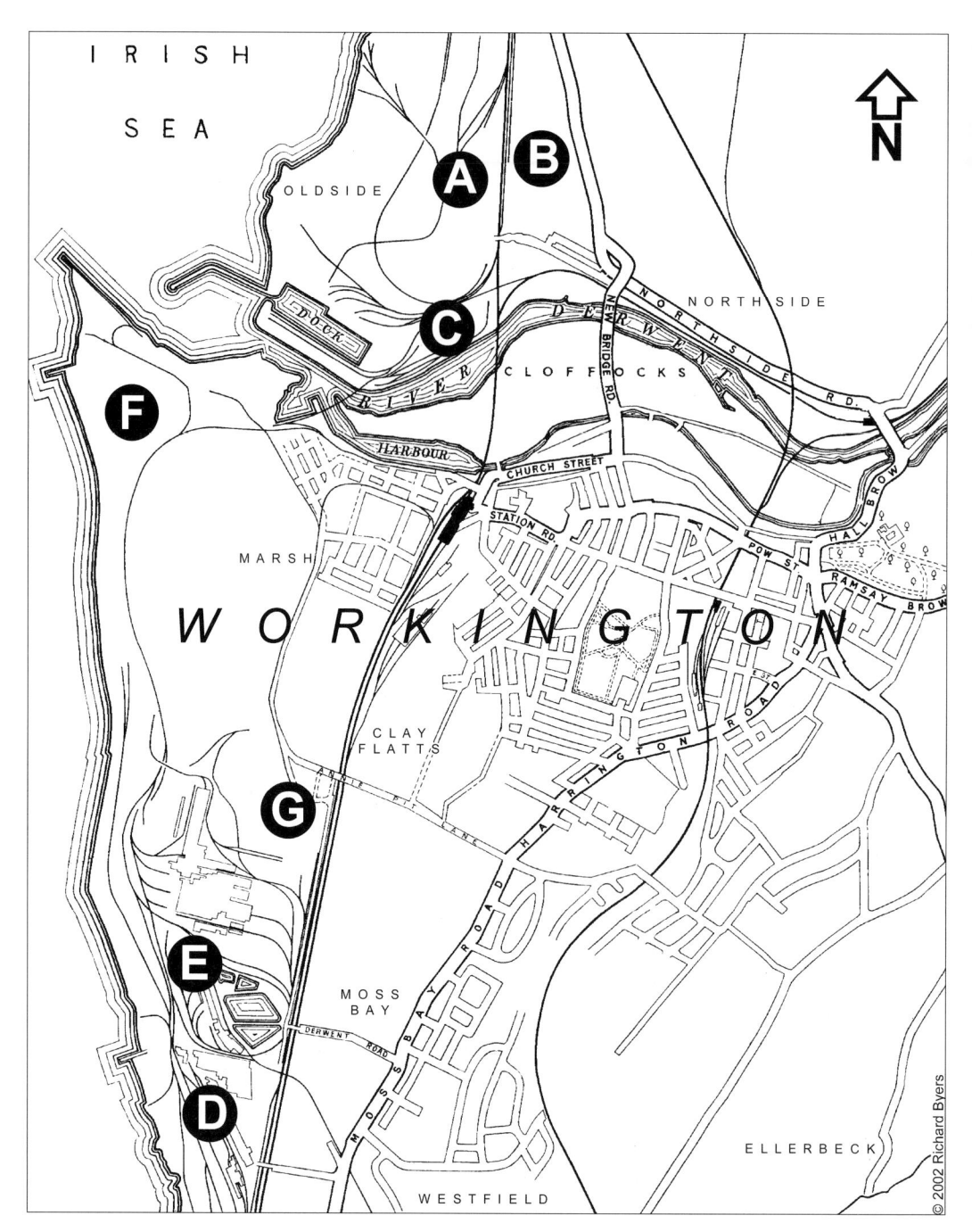

In addition to the Seaton Ironworks at Barepot, there were six other specific sites within the town where iron or steel were manufactured. The location of each works is identified on this map. To assist the reader the Distington Engineering Co. foundry is also indicated. (A) Workington Haematite Iron Co. (B) West Cumberland Haematite Iron Co. (C) North of England Haematite Iron Co. (D) Moss Bay Haematite Iron Co. (E) Derwent Haematite Iron Co. (F) Distington Engineering Co. (G) New Yard Iron Works.

Introduction

During the latter half of the nineteenth century, Workington became a major centre for the production of iron and steel by virtue of its location almost at the centre of the Cumberland coalfield and its close proximity to the rich haematite iron ore deposits which lay between the town and the western fells of the Lake District. The industry grew rapidly from humble beginnings to employ many thousands of people and was primarily responsible for the development and growth of the town and its port. In 1858, Henry Bessemer's revolutionary steel-making process was developed here using the virtually phosphorus-free iron ore mined in the West Cumbrian hills. Bessemer pig iron smelted in the town subsequently became a commodity that was sought after across the world. Several new ironworks were established and their blast furnaces supplied steel plants across Britain, Europe and North America.

Iron production was concentrated on seven sites within the town. The earliest works to manufacture iron on a commercial scale was the Seaton Ironworks at Barepot. Three other ironworks were later established on the north bank of the River Derwent to the west of Barepot at Oldside. These were operated by the Workington Haematite Iron Co., the West Cumberland Haematite Iron Co. and the North of England Haematite Iron Co. (later the Lowther Works). From the mid-1870s, three further plants were built to the south of the river at Moss Bay and Westfield. The first of these was the Moss Bay Haematite Ironworks, on the site currently occupied by Corus Rail. A stone's throw away was the Derwent Ironworks, later acquired by Charles Cammell & Co., whilst a little further to the north was the blast furnace and foundry of the New Yard Ironworks. Initially, each was run as an independent concern until their amalgamation into the Workington Iron & Steel Co. in 1909. A separate chapter in this book is devoted to each of these original ironworks. Their location is clearly identified and the progress and development of the plant recorded. The history and fortunes of the company that first built and operated each site is also plotted, together with details of their successors.

Many of these early ironworks were soon enlarged to also manufacture steel. This expansion was made possible by the rapid growth of the railways, an increase in shipbuilding and expanded trade with North America. Through the skill, ingenuity and tenacity of its workers, major improvements to the steel-making process were made at Workington. The town soon established itself as a centre for steel rail production and throughout its long history has supplied many thousands of miles of track to almost every rail network in the world. Although steel manufacture eventually ceased in the town in 1974, Corus Rail Workington still rolls rails, using basically the same techniques as those described in this book, albeit with the benefit of modern technology. The book concludes with an overview of this once-prominent industry through the last century, including the takeover of the entire Workington operation by the Sheffield-based United Steel Companies and the nationalisation of the industry in 1967.

I wish to acknowledge the invaluable assistance given to me by so many who directly or indirectly contributed to this book. My special thanks are due to Jo Byers, Michael Burridge, Janet Thompson, Eric Hutton, Ray Doran, Joyce Byers, Philip Crouch (Helena Thompson Museum), Edwin George (Corus Rail Workington), the Bessemer Steel Archive, Workington Public Library, Whitehaven and Carlisle Record Offices, and Kelham Island Industrial Museum (Sheffield).

Richard Byers

one

Barepot or Seaton Ironworks

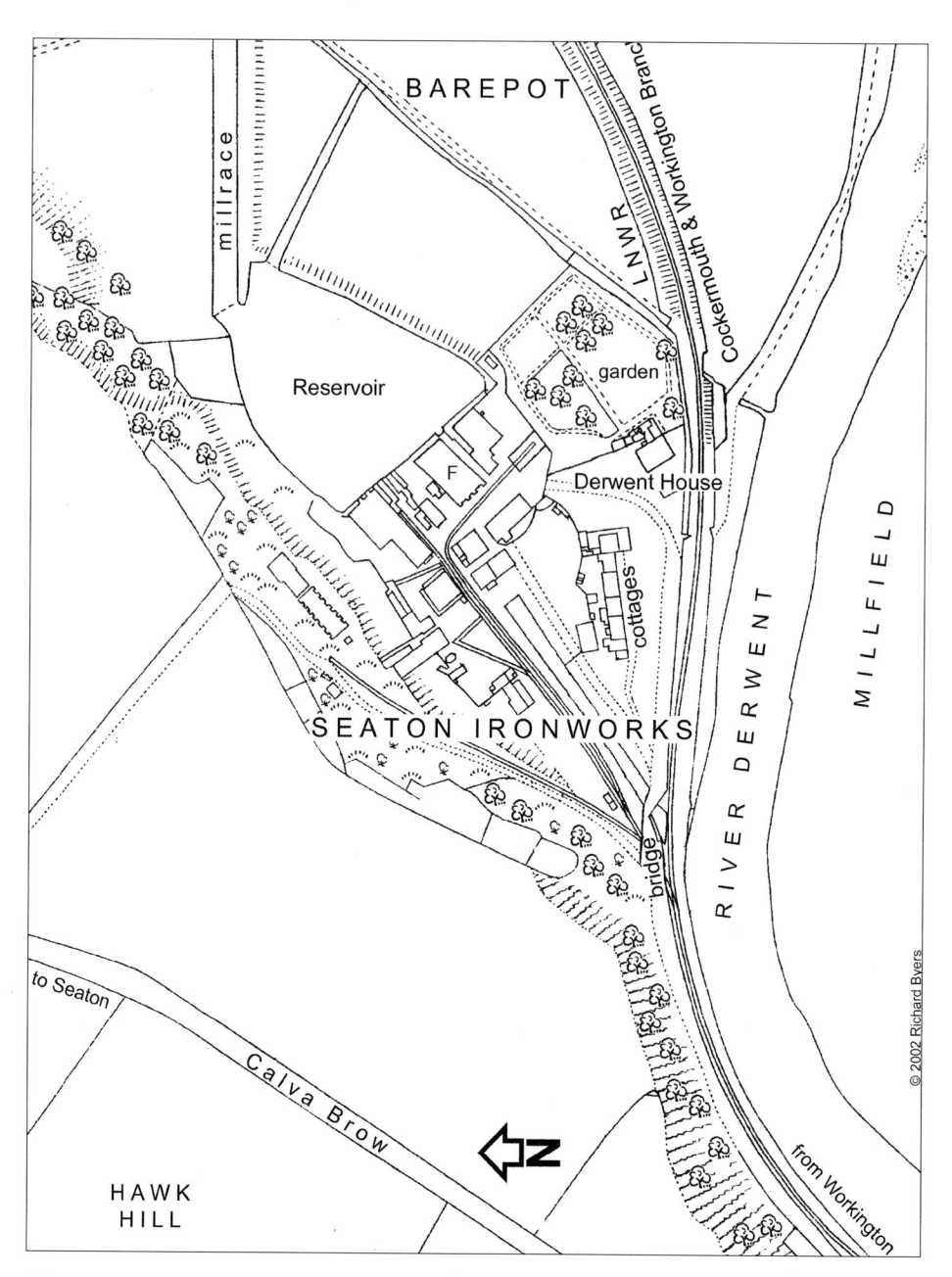

The Seaton Ironworks were located at Barepot, just across the River Derwent from Millfield. Unlike the other ironworks sites within the town which adopted steam power, the early forge, foundry and the blast furnace blowing machine at Barepot were powered by large water wheels. The water was drawn from the river, further upstream (almost opposite Stainburn) and stored in the large reservoir close to the works. Seaton Ironworks also had a connection to the Cockermouth and Workington Railway, opened in April 1847. A succession of works managers are known to have lived in the nearby Derwent House. This substantial detached house had a large secluded walled garden.

Workington's first ironworks was established at Barepot on the north bank of the River Derwent, around a quarter of a mile upstream of Workington Bridge. Here in 1763, William Hicks, Robert Watters, John Ponsonby, William Skyrin and Richard Dearham are said to have built what became generally known as Seaton Ironworks. The site at 'Barepotts meadow and Holegill' was leased from the Lowther family. Hutchinson, in his 1794 *History of Cumberland*, tells us that the 'eminent engineer' Thomas Spedding (of Whitehaven) was also actively involved in the enterprise. He is credited with planning and building the works, which included one of the first blast furnaces in Cumberland. However, other records suggest it was actually James Spedding (1720–88) who established the works. Despite this confusion we do know that the ironworks then traded as Spedding, Hicks & Co.

The French metallurgist Gabriel Jars visited Seaton Ironworks in 1765 and wrote an extremely valuable description of the plant. He noted that one blast furnace was then in production, with another under construction. The pig iron maufactured at Barepot was then virtually all converted into quality wrought iron. Wrought iron is almost pure iron produced by reheating pig iron in a puddling furnace to oxidise away the impurities. The iron ore used at the works was noted as being the same as that smelted at Clifton. Sugden in his 1897 *History of Arlecdon & Frizington* added this was brought over land by packhorse from the Frizington district.

The fuel used in this first Barepot blast furnace was charcoal, thought to have been brought south from Scotland. But Jars also mentions that it was planned to fire the new furnace with coke, to produce only cast iron. Unless the coke supplies were to be purchased elsewhere, it is not exactly clear how this coke was to be produced. Perhaps they were to adopt a similar method to that used at nearby Clifton; here, heaps of coal were laid upon a thick base of sandstone slabs, then it was covered with earth and set alight. By adjusting the rate of combustion, the heap of coal was reduced in much the same way as charcoal is traditionally produced from timber.

John Mordy's early engraving of Seaton ironworks (c.1850) viewed from Millfield on the opposite side of the River Derwent. The long row of workers' terraced cottages can be seen in the foreground, with Derwent House to the right. Up on the hillside in the distance are the coke ovens. (Joyce Byers Collection)

By 1794, Hutchinson provided some further details of the Barepot works, which by then had obviously expanded. There were still two blast furnaces, but in addition there was:

> a mill for slitting and rolling bar iron, a double forge for refining and drawing of bar iron, a foundry with several small furnaces, wherein they make cannon and cast iron work of all sorts; a boring mill for boring cannon cylinders, etc., a grinding house and turning house and many other conveniences suitable for carrying on very extensive iron manufacturing.

Coke was also now produced on site in a row of four or five beehive shaped coke ovens, located on the hillside overlooking the works.

From around 1775 until after the Napoleonic wars, Seaton Ironworks is known to have manufactured many cannons. At the time all English shipping was in constant danger of attack, not just from the hostile French and American navies, but also from marauding pirate ships, even close to home in the Solway Firth. It now became standard practice for the Workington shipbuilders to add cannons to their new ships, and there is little doubt the ironworks supplied many of these. Several contemporary newspaper advertisements tell how the cannons cast by Spedding, Hicks & Co. could be 'test fired in the presence of any person the purchaser may appoint'. It is said that they were loaded and fired across the River Derwent into the hillside below Stainburn.

The works then employed several hundred local people, busily producing castings and iron work of all descriptions. The advertisements also proudly boast that they could manufacture almost any 'article in the Cast Iron way, in the neatest manner, and on the lowest terms'. Although their largest customers were likely to be the local shipbuilders and collieries, to whom they supplied items such as bar iron, bogie wheels, nails, hoops, pistons and cylinders, boiler plates and barrow wheels, Barepot also manufactured an extensive range of general household items such as frying pans, griddles, pye pans, tea kettles, clothes irons, stoves and grates. The general public could purchase these by calling at the Barepot works or from their warehouse in Whitehaven.

By 1791, the company was trading as Spedding, Hicks, Senhouse & Co., and had begun to manufacture and assemble the Heslop Rotary Steam Engine. Invented by a local man, Adam Heslop, the design was patented in July 1790. Around twenty of these engines are known to have been built and installed in the West Cumberland coal pits. It is thought Heslop become an employee at the Barepot, perhaps to supervise the construction of his engine. The works may well have then manufactured his first steam engines under licence. Unfortunately, there is no record of the actual arrangement he had with the proprietors. In 1798, Heslop resigned in order to continue to build his engines elsewhere, forming a new company Heslop, Milward & Co. He later erected their own new foundry at Lowca, near Harrington, leasing the land from John Christian Curwen.

In August 1813, a further advertisement in the *Cumberland Pacquet* tells us that the Seaton company had recently 'extended their Brass & Cast Iron foundry', but the actual extent of this work is not recorded in any detail. However, it is revealed that they were now also manufacturing 'stoves for churches, shops, ships etc. [and] Cast iron ploughs'. Yet just over a year later, the works were advertised for sale. From the auction particulars we learn that Barepot now consisted of 'a blast furnace capable of making thirty to forty tons of iron per week', said to have been substantially rebuilt the previous year, together with 'ovens for coking coal, a large foundry or moulding house for both iron and brass, a double forge, refineries and slitting and rolling mill'. It was now being sold by the proprietors, Spedding, Dickinson, Russell & Co. It was suggested that its principal partners now wished to retire, but in truth it was more likely that activity at the works had been decline for some time. As no financial accounts of the company have survived, the true state of the business remains a mystery.

Certainly, the likelihood of poor profits may explain why no purchaser was forthcoming. Finally, at the beginning of June 1819, the company was sold at

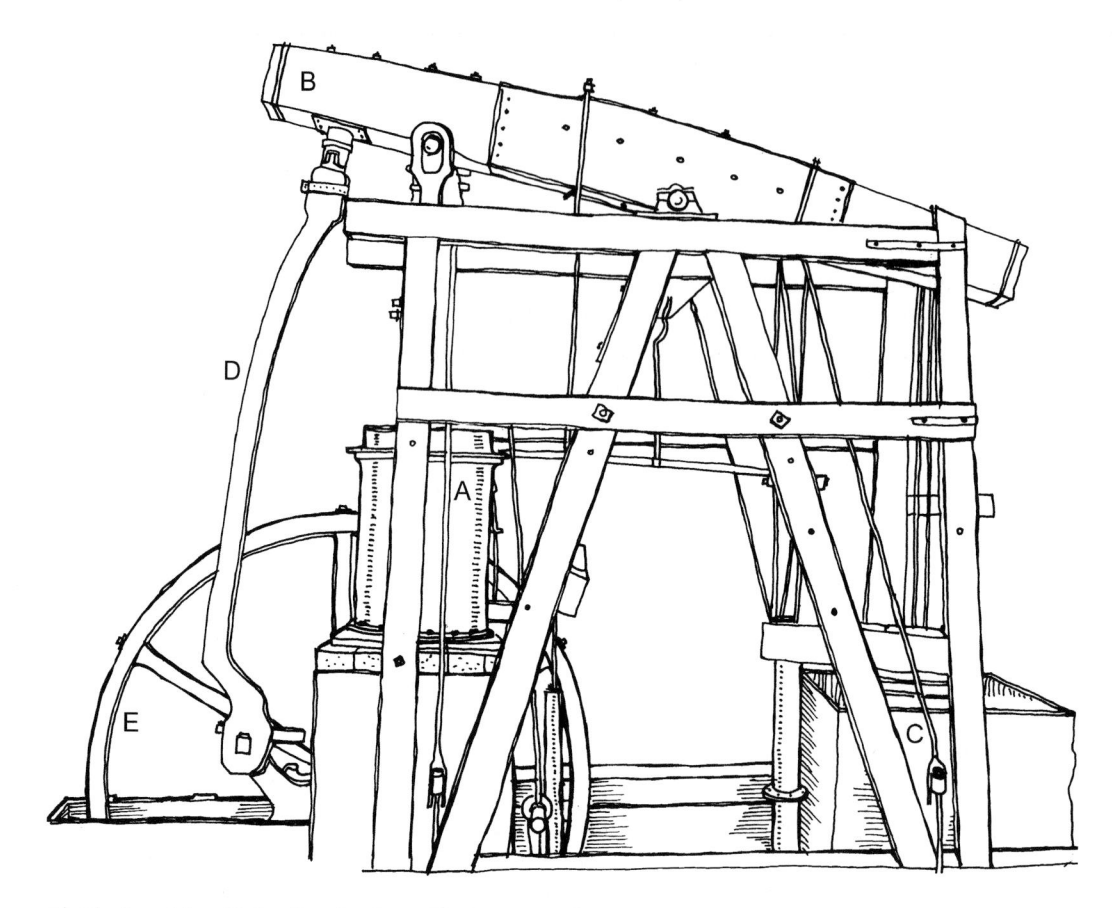

Sketch of an Adam Heslop Rotative Steam Engine, patented in 1790 and built at the Seaton Ironworks. This illustration is based on the engine which was installed at Low Wreah Pit, Whitehaven, and later acquired by the Science Museum. Heslop's invention did not infringe James Watt's earlier and more famous steam engine patent as it adopted two cylinders (A and C) at either end of the main beam. Steam from an adjacent boiler (not shown above) is admitted into the hot (or receiving) cylinder A, forcing the main beam B to rise at that side. A valve then opens allowing the steam to pass to the cold (or working) cylinder C. The reducing pressure in A and the rising pressure in C now forces the beam down. As cylinder C is immersed in cold water, the steam condenses, thus creating a vacuum and drawing that end of the beam downward. The rocking motion of the main beam turns the flywheel E, via the connecting rod D.

auction to Heslop, Milward, Johnson & Co. So Adam Heslop, who had left the Seaton Ironworks over twenty years earlier to set up a new foundry at Lowca, now returned to take control of his old workplace. Adam was in partnership with his brothers Crosby and Thomas Heslop. Again few records survive to tell us more about the new owners of Barepot, although the Heslop family gravestone in St Michael's Church records that all three brothers had died by Christmas 1835.

Around 1837, Seaton Ironworks was sold again, this time to Tulk, Ley & Co. They also purchased Heslop's Lowca Ironworks, suggesting that both concerns may have been purchased from the Heslops' executors. That same year, Tulk and Ley took a lease on the iron ore pits at Yeathouse (Frizington). Obviously, now owning their own blast furnaces, they would wish to secure a cheap and constant supply of iron ore. Lancaster and Wattleworth tell us the partnership was made up of John Augustus Tulk (the principal shareholder) and James Peard Ley (of Bideford). Despite major partnership problems, the company appears to have continued to operate the Barepot works until around 1851. During this period they may have also rebuilt and upgraded its blast furnace, and added a rail connection into the plant from the newly opened Cockermouth & Workington Railway. There are no records of their output at Seaton Ironworks, but we know that in 1849 they mined around 15,000 tons of iron ore from their two pits at Yeathouse.

From 1852, the plant was taken over by the partnership of Messrs Henderson & Davis. They were known to have converted and adapted Barepot for tinplate production. Tinplate was made by repeatedly reheating and rolling wrought-iron bars into thin sheets, then coating their surfaces with a film of tin. The tin protected the iron against rusting and corrosion. They also erected the Quayside Ironworks on the south side of Stanley Street, next to where the gasworks was built. It was sometimes also called the Derwent Ironworks and later the Derwent Tinplate Works. It had no connection with the later and much larger Derwent Haematite Iron Co. at Moss Bay, which began production in 1875.

By 1860, Seaton Ironworks employed 120 men and Lancaster & Wattleworth tell us it was then operated by Samuel Wagstaffe Smith. For the next five years Smith continued tinplate production and is also known to have resumed smelting iron. Within twelve months the workforce had increased to nearly 195. But work was not continuous, for in June 1861 they were all laid off 'in consequence of a stagnation of trade'. Without doubt, the establishment of the larger and more technologically advanced blast furnaces at Oldside spelt the end of iron making at Barepot. From 1865 to 1870, the plant is believed to have been run by Samuel Sandys Briggs. The former ironworks at Seaton was then finally acquired by William Ivander Griffiths and given over entirely to tinplate production.

A 1999 aerial photograph of the former Seaton Ironworks site at Barepot, viewed from the south-east. The only remaining feature of the works is the large reservoir in the centre, which once powered several waterwheels at the plant. Water was drawn upstream from the River Derwent along the mill race to the extreme right of the photograph, seen running parallel to the road.

two

Workington Haematite Iron Co.
Workington Haematite Iron & Steel Co.
Workington Iron Co.
Oldside Iron and Steel Works

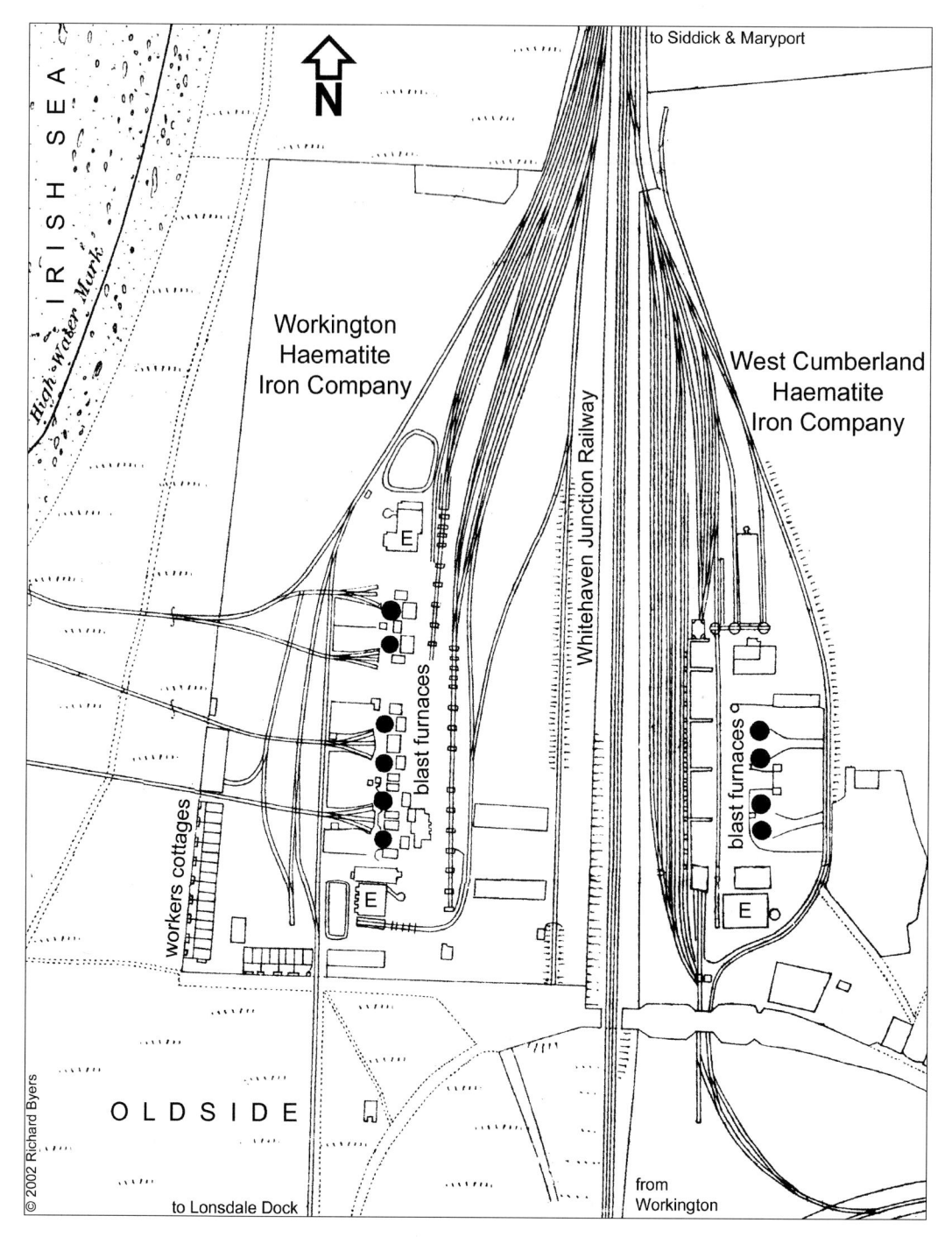

Map showing both the layout of the Workington Haematite Ironworks and the adjoining West Cumberland Haematite Ironworks around 1863. These two quite independent companies were located north of the River Derwent at Oldside, on either side of the Whitehaven Junction Railway line to Maryport. This track, eventually acquired by the London & North Western Railway, is shown almost in the centre of the map running from the top to the bottom of the page.

The Workington Haematite Iron Co. works which began production in February 1958, was located to the north of the River Derwent estuary at Oldside. It occupied a relatively narrow strip of land between the shoreline and the main railway line north to Maryport. The site is identified on the location plan on p.6 by the letter A. This new limited company had been incorporated in November 1856 with a share capital of £250,000, consisting of fifty £500 shares. Initially just two blast furnaces were constructed to the south of the site. These early blast furnaces, or skiddies as they were sometimes called, were constructed almost entirely of masonry and lined with firebrick. They had open tops which allowed the waste gases and heat to freely escape.

A contemporary account of the works tells us that there was also a large 'heavy quadrangular building' housing a massive 200hp steam engine. This vast beam engine provided the powerful air blast into each furnace; it had a 22ft (6.7m) diameter flywheel, which alone weighed around 15 tons. The beam itself was at least 36ft (11m) long, and gracefully rocked as the cylinders moved at up to sixteen strokes per minute, forcing 18,000 cubic feet of air into the base of the furnaces. The scale of this steam engine is now quite difficult to comprehend. Its basic appearance would have been very similar to Heslop's earlier engine (see p.14), although it was much larger and it was technically more refined. The works also had around sixty-six small coke ovens, built to the 'newest and most approved principles'. Each was capable of converting around six tons of coal. Built around the south-west corner of the site were the offices, stables and two rows of terraced workers' cottages.

Within two years, two further stone blast furnaces had been added and the site employed around 100 men. Initially the works were built and managed under the supervision of a Mr Thorburn. Later, Joseph Smith held the post for almost twenty years, until the plant was sold around 1879. Work on building two additional blast furnaces and a further additional powerful steam engine began in the spring of 1860. The new ironworks also had a connection to the Whitehaven Junction Railway and a further line looping south to link the plant to the new Lonsdale Dock.

A sketch of the Workington Haematite Ironworks at Oldside, based on an engraving of c.1860. The works then employed around 100 people. The row of six brick-built blast furnaces or 'skiddies' are viewed from the south-west corner of the plant. During ironmaking, the gas produced was then allowed to escape freely and be burned off at the top of these early open-topped structures. Within a decade, the efficiency of the blast furnace was greatly improved when it was closed off at the top and the waste gases and lost heat were recirculated back to the foot of the furnace.

The tall building to the right of the picture housed a massive 200hp steam engine. This vast beam engine provided the powerful air blast to the foot of each furnace. Records tell us that its huge flywheel measured 22ft (6.7m) in diameter, and weighed around 15 tons. The beam itself was at least 36ft (11m) long and gracefully rocked as the cylinders moved at up to sixteen strokes per minute, forcing around 18,000 cubic feet of air to the base of the furnaces. The tall brick chimney of the adjoining boiler house was around 125ft (38m) high and had an internal diameter of 6ft 6in (2m). A similar engine house and chimney was also built at the opposite end of the row of blast furnaces and can be seen in the distance.

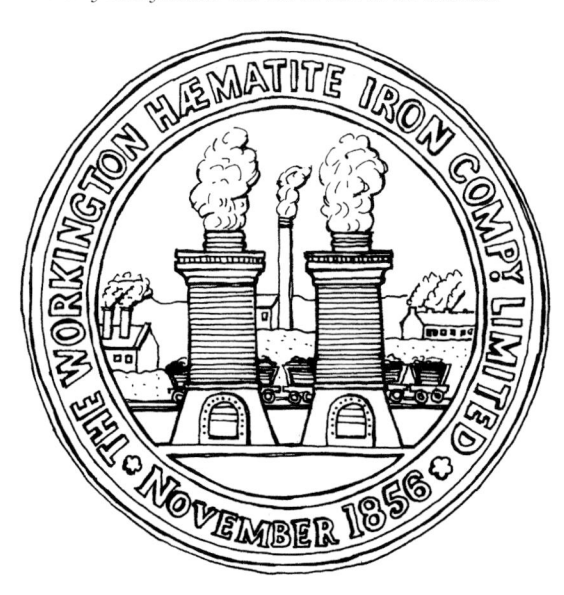

Sketch of the Workington Haematite Iron Co. roundel from a plaque at the Moss Bay Bessemer Training School. The date the company was first incorporated is recorded and two of the older-style open-topped blast furnaces are depicted. The initial share capital of the Workington Haematite Iron Co. was £25,000, consisting of fifty £500 shares.

It was at this Workington ironworks that the prolific inventor Henry Bessemer (1813–1898) finally discovered an ideal source of quality pig iron to use in his revolutionary new steel-making process. In 1855, he had discovered that by blowing a blast of air through molten pig iron he could oxidise away its naturally occurring impurities to create steel. He soon realised his invention could be scaled up to manufacture larger quantities of relatively cheap steel with very little effort. Until then, such a process had been impossible.

Today, we take steel very much for granted. But as Bessemer comments in his autobiography, before he made his discovery 'there was no steel suitable for structural purposes; ships, bridges, railway rails, tyres and axles were constructed of wrought iron'. The use of steel was then confined to 'cutlery, tools, springs, and the smaller parts of machinery', as its manufacture was 'long and costly'.

Henry Bessemer came to Oldside soon after starting to build his Sheffield steel works, which opened in 1858. He was fully aware that West Cumberland mines produced 'the purest iron ore which this country possessed'. But there was a problem with the quality of pig iron then produced from Workington's blast furnaces. He was surprised to find that the smelted iron had a high phosphorus content, making it unsuitable for his process. Bessemer toured the works, taking samples for analysis of all the raw materials, and discussed the problem with furnace managers. Initially, it was a mystery how such pure iron ore could become contaminated during processing. Then he discovered that the flux (or cinder) added to aid the blast furnace operation contained the phosphoric impurities. This flux was in fact a 'reddish brown furnace waste' brought from Staffordshire as ballast in empty ships returning to Workington harbour. The ironworks had previously found this material quite suitable, as well as no doubt extremely cheap. Bessemer simply switched to another flux, and later wrote: 'I now feel certain we would soon have thousands of tons of British iron suitable for the production of steel by my process'.

Suddenly, this virtually phosphorus-free 'Bessemer pig iron' became a much sought-after commodity and the company grew rapidly. The subsequent enormous worldwide demand for steel products brought a boom period to the town and its ironworks. Workington pig iron contributed to the building of new railway facilities, the construction of iron ships and the trade with America, Germany and Italy. Obviously, it also benefited the town's port, the local iron ore and coal mines and the railway companies.

By 1871, the Workington Haematite Iron Co. (often referred to locally as the 'Old company') employed around 300 men. But boom times are inevitably followed by slumps and the town's first major ironworks was forced to cease production around 1874. Newspaper records tells us that the ironworks then held 'an enormous stock of pig-iron', but were forced to sell at 'much below the cost of manufacture'. The disheartened directors formally wound up the company. Their long-serving manager, Joseph Smith, who had run the works for almost fifteen years, was also forced to retire due to his failing eyesight. Six

An engraving showing several portraits of Henry Bessemer (1813–98). He invented his revolutionary steel-making process in 1855, enabling large quantities of steel to be produced at minimal cost, a process which was developed and refined at Workington. Today, we take steel very much for granted, but before the Bessemer process there was simply no steel suitable for structural purposes, such as ships, girders, bridges or railways. It was then only ever used for cutlery, hand tools, springs and other small machine parts.

idle years followed, before the works were eventually sold to the Workington Haematite Iron & Steel Co., a new joint stock company. Amongst its new directors were Charles James Valentine, Peter Kirk, Joseph Ledger, and Peter G. Quirk. These men would play a prominent part in the history of iron and steel manufacture in Workington.

By June 1877, all but two of the six now obsolete stone blast furnaces or skiddies had been demolished. Two were later rebuilt with about double the capacity of their predecessors. Their design had been greatly improved and each was now enclosed at the top, in order to recycle the previously lost gases and heat. Pig iron was smelted once again here during the first weeks of 1880 and the two remaining original blast furnaces, adjacent to the southern engine house, were converted to smelt spiegel. Spiegel (or spiegeleisen) is an alloy of iron, manganese and carbon used during the Bessemer process to create a particular grade of steel.

A fresh impetus in the Bessemer pig iron trade brought a further period of relative prosperity which lasted three or four years. In September 1882, a further new blast furnace was brought into service at the Oldside works. By then, the Cumberland furnaces were responsible for smelting 12 per cent of the UK's pig iron. In 1901, the company was formally wound up and the plant was acquired by the Workington Iron Co. This new company, formed in 1900, had a share capital of £337,500 and its directors included Joseph Ellis, Sir John Scurrah Randles and Herbert Valentine, all of whom were also directors of the Moss Bay Haematite Iron & Steel Co. The three remaining blast furnaces were then almost entirely given over to the production of spiegel and ferro-manganese.

Some periods of inactivity followed until 1909, when the works were absorbed into the newly established Workington Iron & Steel Co. Because of possible confusion with the new company, the name of the old Workington ironworks was changed to the Oldside Iron & Steelworks. A 1929 aerial photograph of the Prince of Wales dock exists which clearly shows the works to the north of the harbour. There is no smoke evident from the row of towering blast furnaces, suggesting production was again at a standstill. By the winter of 1933, it is believed that only one of the remaining three furnaces was still in use. This too was shut down soon afterwards; local newspaper reports show that work to demolish the 'long abandoned blast furnaces at Oldside' began in the spring of 1934.

The former Workington Haematite Iron & Steel Co. works at Oldside (c.1910), viewed from the south west. Only three of the six original blast furnaces then remained and these were used principally to smelt spiegel or ferro-manganese alloys. At the rear of the furnaces, to the right, is a row of shorter hot-blast regenerative stoves. Within these cylindrical structures, the waste gases from the top of the blast furnace were recycled to pre-heat the blast of air used to smelt the iron (see p.83). Once the plant was transferred to the Workington Iron & Steel Co. in 1909, the works were renamed the Oldside Iron and Steel Works.

three

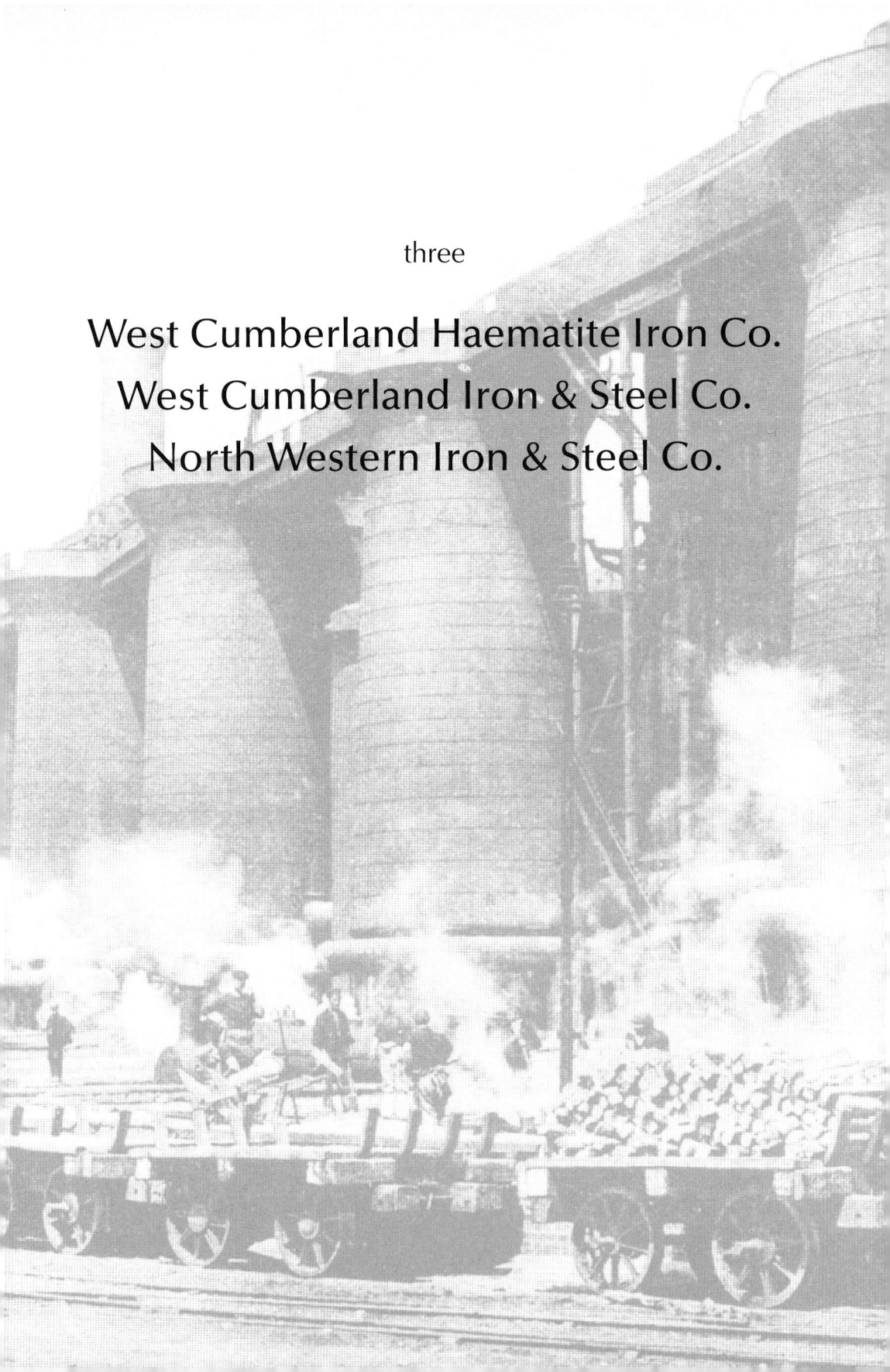

West Cumberland Haematite Iron Co.
West Cumberland Iron & Steel Co.
North Western Iron & Steel Co.

Above: *The six blast furnaces of the West Cumberland Iron & Steel works, c.1889, viewed from the north-west corner of the site. The molten iron was tapped from the base of the furnaces on this side of the site and allowed to flow into pig beds immediately in front of the furnaces. To the right is the main hoist used to lift the raw materials to the platform running across the top of the furnaces.*

Right: *George James Snelus (1837–1906), the accomplished metallurgist and chemist who was appointed the first manager of the West Cumberland Iron & Steel Co. in 1872. He had previously been the chief chemist at Glamorgan's Dowlais Iron and Steel Works. Perhaps his greatest achievement was the invention of the 'basic' furnace linings. This allowed quality steel to be made from inferior ore and pig iron, containing a previously unacceptable phosphorus level. Although initially intended for the Bessemer converter, his innovative 'basic' lining was more extensively used in Sydney Thomas' open hearth process of steelmaking.*

The West Cumberland Haematite Iron Co. was also located to the north of the Derwent estuary at Oldside. It was situated immediately opposite the Workington Haematite Ironworks on the other side of the the main railway line north to Maryport. The site is identified on the plan on p.6 by the letter B. This new company was created to take advantage of the growing worldwide demand for Workington's Bessemer pig iron. Work began on the site in March 1860, with the construction of four blast furnaces. Their design differed significantly from the open-topped skiddies of their neighbours on the opposite side of the railway. Instead of the massive masonry structure, these blast furnaces were now almost totally encased in thick steel plate. The hot gases that belched out from the earlier models were now recirculated to the foot of the structure to pre-heat the air blast. These new furnaces benefited greatly from recent advances in technology. The quality of the smelted iron was now much better regulated and controlled, with production here being far more economical and cost-effective than older furnaces. Much of the initial building work was carried out by Messrs Telford. Along the southern edge of the site were twelve workers' cottages built for the company in the summer of 1860 by Mr Frazer of Harrington. The first pig iron was smelted here in November 1862.

In October 1864, a new extensive plate-rolling mill was added to the north of the ironworks. During the construction work, which lasted around eight months, two gigantic steam engine flywheels (each 25ft in diameter and weighing around 28 tons) were cast on site. Newspaper reports tell us that it was thought to be 'the largest casting ever attempted in Cumberland', and the rim of each flywheel was said to be 'as fine as if it were turned on a lathe'. One can easily forget the problems and logistics of building such heavy machinery in Victorian times; work of this kind would still present mammoth problems for today's engineers. The extended works were officially opened by Isaac Fletcher (of Tarn Bank) on 23 May 1865, when he set in motion the two large steam engines. The finishing rollers of the plate mill were 7ft long and 24in in diameter, and said to be capable of producing 1,400 tons of finished plate a week. The plant now covered eight acres and had thirty-two new puddling furnaces.

With the company now producing around 2,000 tons of Bessemer-quality pig iron each week, their next obvious step for the ironworks was an expansion into steel-making. In 1872, the directors restructured the company, changing its name to the West Cumberland Haematite Iron & Steel Co. They raised the necessary capital by issuing £600,000-worth of new shares. Their prospectus boasted that 'the works was more eligibly placed for the manufacture of Bessemer steel, than any other'. The transfer to the new company was completed on 30 September 1872, and the shareholders of the old company received around £485,000. The balance was used to fund the building of the new steel plant, with four 7½-ton Bessemer converters and a rail mill. Construction work had actually begun during the autumn of 1870 and the first steel was cast in mid-November 1872. Much of this early steel from the West Cumberland works was cast into large bars or ingots, then rolled into flat plates and railway lines.

George James Snelus (1837–1906) was appointed as the first manager of the company's new steel-making department. He was a distinguished metallurgist and chemist, who had travelled extensively and had closely studied iron and steel production on both sides of the Atlantic. By the time he arrived in Workington, this relatively young man had already achieved significant success. Revd Edward Haigh Sugden (George Snelus' parish priest at Arlecdon) tells us in his *History of Arlecdon and Frizington* that he 'laid the foundations of his success by his preliminary study of chemistry and metallurgy, being a student of Professor Roscoe, at Owen's College, Manchester'. In 1864, he gained the first Albert Scholarship, which entitled him to '£50 per annum and free education for three years at the Royal School of Mines'. His success here was outstanding; he was the top student for each of his three years, and became an associate in mining and metallurgy. Upon leaving college, Snelus was appointed the chief chemist at the Glamorgan Dowlais Iron & Steel Works. The prestigious Iron & Steel Institute later invited him to travel to America as the scientific member of their investigation into Danks' mechanical process of puddling. During this visit he also took the opportunity to note any important developments in the American steel industry. Lancaster and Wattleworth, in their history of the industry in West Cumbria, commented that this 'was to serve him well in his future appointment' at Workington.

Perhaps his greatest achievement was the innovative use of dolomitic or magnesitic 'basic' furnace linings. This invention, patented in 1872, now allowed quality steel to be made from inferior ore and re-used pig iron containing a previously unacceptably high phosphorus content. Although initially intended for the Bessemer converter, his basic linings were more extensively used in the Sydney Thomas' open hearth process of steel-making. Henry Bessemer did eventually adopted the Snelus linings for his own converters. For this discovery, Snelus received the Bessemer Gold Medal from the Iron & Steel Institute in 1883. Sugden tells us that 'the first piece of steel ever made by this process' was still preserved by its inventor in 1897. One wonders what happened to the treasured memento of the process by which many hundreds of millions of tons of steel have since been made. He then lived virtually alone at Ennerdale Hall (near Arlecdon), indulging his hobby of growing rare orchids. Seldom was he ever seen in public without one of his floral specimens proudly displayed in the buttonhole of his jacket.

Within a very short time, George Snelus was appointed general manager of the entire West Cumberland works and his knowledge was to prove vital to the survival of the company. By the end of 1874, the period of unexampled prosperity ended and the industry slid into a long recession. Over a four-year

Ironworkers tap the molten iron from the foot of a row of blast furnaces, allowing it to flow into the sand-lined pig beds. This was a typical activity undertaken several times every day when the West Cumberland Iron & Steel Works was in full production. The plant was one of the first to also transport molten pig iron directly to their Bessemer converters. During the early 1880s, they were producing around 3,500 tons of steel rails each week.

Above: *An engraving of an enlarged view of the foot of an early West Cumberland Ironworks blast furnace. The blast of air into the furnace was carried in a horseshoe-shaped blast main (A), which encircled the structure except at the front. This was an iron pipe lined internally with fire-brick, and supported about 8ft (2.4m) above the ground level. From this larger diameter main, smaller vertical pipes (B) at regular intervals conveyed the blast through several tuyère blocks (C) built into the foot of the furnace. The tuyères or air holes in the later blast furnaces were all water-cooled, particularly after the practice of pre-heating the blast was introduced.*

Opposite: *An engraving of a cross-section through a typical blast furnace at the West Cumberland Iron & Steel Works, c.1890. Into the hollow centre of these tall structures the basic raw materials of ironmaking were dropped. These were iron or haematite ore, the fuel (coke) and a flux. A massive air blast was then introduced to the foot of the furnace generating intense heat. This melted and fused the contents together, the molten iron gathering within the foot of the furnace. This was then drawn off and allowed to flow into pig iron moulds (or beds), where it solidified. Each furnace was refilled regularly and kept alight or 'in blast' almost continuously. Unlike the open-topped brick built furnaces of the Workington Haematite Ironworks, these were encased in thick steel plates. At the top the opening was closed off with a conical-shaped plug, which could be lowered to allow the furnaces to be refilled. The waste heat and gases were recirculated back to the foot of the structure and used to pre-heat the air blast.* (Michael Burridge Collection)

period, steel prices fell by a massive 65 per cent and both the Workington Haematite Iron Co. and Lowther Ironworks were forced to close. During these difficult times, Snelus' innovation greatly reduced the company's overheads, increased its efficiency and even maintained a modest profit. In 1875-6, rather than rebuilding three of the older blast furnaces at the West Cumberland works, the company extensively repaired and remodelled them. Each was raised by 15ft (4.6m) to around 70ft (21m) in height. The company, which already owned its own limestone quarry at Brigham, also acquired Clifton Colliery to guarantee supplies of coal for coking. Their representatives also exhibited at the Paris Exhibition of 1878, where they achieved remarkable success, winning gold medals for their exhibits of haematite pig iron, Bessemer steel ingots, castings,

Cubic Contents 10388 Feet.

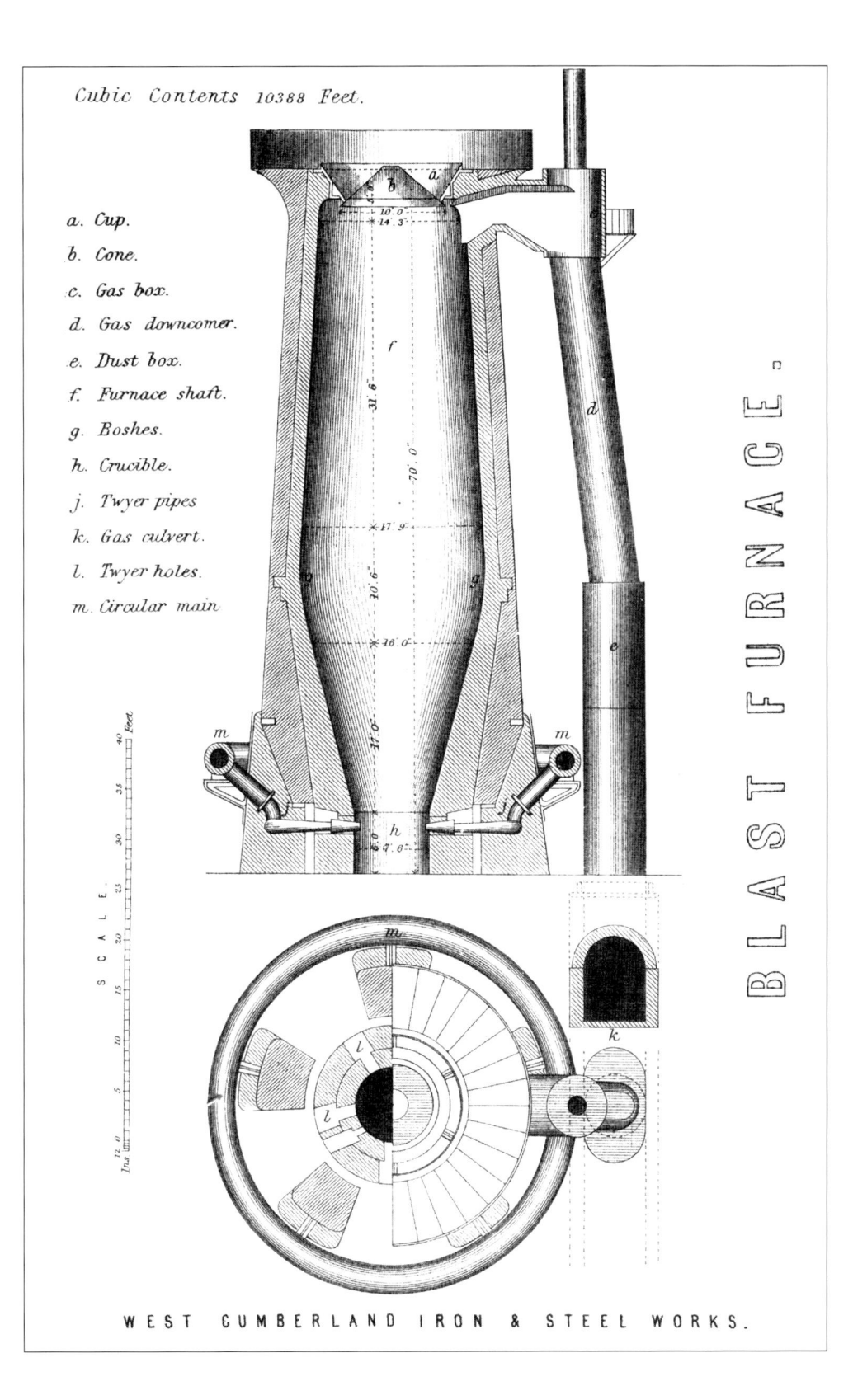

a. Cup.
b. Cone.
c. Gas box.
d. Gas downcomer.
e. Dust box.
f. Furnace shaft.
g. Boshes.
h. Crucible.
j. Twyer pipes
k. Gas culvert.
l. Twyer holes.
m. Circular main

BLAST FURNACE.

WEST CUMBERLAND IRON & STEEL WORKS.

rails and plates. Promoting their products at such international exhibitions brought vital export orders to the West Cumberland works.

We know from the writings of Henry Fraser Curwen that by the end of 1879 the heavy industries of West Cumberland were beginning to recover. 'Iron prices were very high again and the iron ore mines and coal pits were again scenes of activity.' Within a few months, all six blast furnaces at the West Cumberland works were once more 'in blast', as production of pig iron rose once again. The rail mills were also subsequently remodelled to allow the manufacture of both steel and boiler plate. In June 1883, a new cast-iron blast furnace was blown in at the works. Built on eight massive columns, the 70ft-high structure was capable of producing 1,000 tons of pig iron each week. Just five months later, a further blast furnace was recommissioned after being totally rebuilt. The West Cumberland works were then described as by far the largest concern in the town. The works now extended for around 1 mile north towards Siddick. By 1883, they employed over 1,400 local people, had six blast furnaces and produced 3,000–4,000 tons of steel rails each week.

Yet the iron and steel industry was still riding a rollercoaster of boom and bust. By 1888, a serious slump had intervened again. Despite its best efforts, the company was forced into liquidation in December 1888. It was ten months before it began trading once more. During the next couple of years, parts of the plant were closed and workers were laid off during several periods of inactivity. Finally in May 1892, the directors agreed to wind up the company and attempt to dispose of the works, although newspaper reports suggest they saw little prospect of a sale during a recession described as 'the very worst in the history of iron and steel in West Cumberland'.

Nearly seven years after closure, the now dilapidated and abandoned West Cumberland works were eventually sold to the North Western Iron & Steel Co. Formed in 1898, this new company overhauled and modernised much of the old West Cumberland ironworks, and expected production to recommence in spring the following year. Initially, just two of the five remaining blast furnaces were restarted, with the other three put in blast during the following year or so. However, this enterprise was very short-lived as, by July 1902, the entire works was closed and advertised for sale. No purchaser was forthcoming and the once-thriving works was dismantled soon afterwards.

four

North of England Haematite Iron Co.
Lowther Haematite Iron Co.
Lowther Haematite Iron & Steel Co.

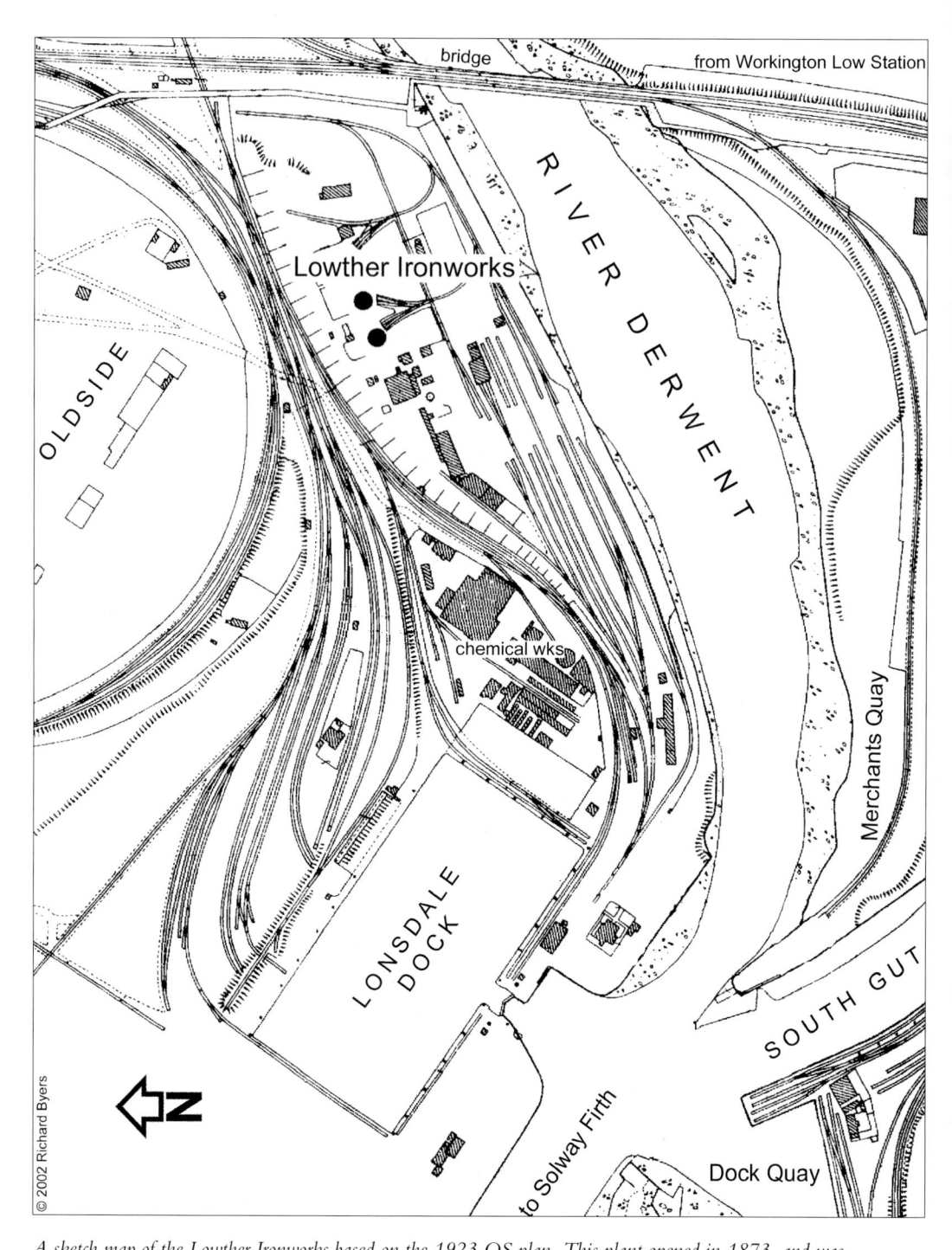

A sketch map of the Lowther Ironworks based on the 1923 OS plan. This plant opened in 1873, and was located on the north bank of the River Derwent, just to the east of Lonsdale Dock. Part of the site had previously been used as a wharf for the Seaton Ironworks. The Lonsdale Dock (opened in 1861) was eventually replaced by the present Prince of Wales Dock (opened in 1927).

The North of England Haematite Ironworks was located on the north bank of the River Derwent midway between the Lonsdale Dock and Whitehaven Junction Railway bridge across the river. The site is identified on the plan on p.6 by the letter C. This new company was formed by Andrew Barclay (of Kilmarnock) and David George Hoey (of Lanark), who were granted a 99-year lease of the land in May 1872. Their ironworks was ideally situated, close to both the dock and railways. The local newspaper tells us that work on building the new works began in August 1872. Within ten months, the first blast furnace was completed and blown in. That first year the company made a respectable £17,000 profit. On paper the Scotsmen made a perfect team; Barclay provided the technical knowledge, while Hoey, an accountant, handled the financial management. But unfortunately, after an encouraging start, they too were seriously affected by the major recession of mid 1870s, and the North of England Haematite Iron Co. was subsequently forced into liquidation.

For six months, the creditors allowed production to continue at the works whilst the company fullfilled outstanding orders. During this time they lost the services of the works manager, Hugh Jamieson (1839–75), who died suddenly in March 1875. By June, they accepted that the workers must be laid off and the two furnaces dampened down. As the bankrupt ironworks lay idle, talks and negotiations continued for several months. Finally in October, it was purchased by the Lowther Haematite Iron Co., a new joint-stock company with a capital of £250,000. After negotiations with his creditors, David George Hoey made a surprise return as a director of the new business. Almost immediately, both the blast furnaces were restarted. But this was still a particularly difficult period for the iron industry and during 1879 production was often halted for long periods. It appears that during this stoppage at least two of the blast furnaces were increased in height and remodelled. In January 1880, William Wilson, the former secretary of the nearby West Cumberland Iron & Steel Co., joined the board of the Lowther Ironworks. One of his first tasks was to restart pig iron production, signalling the reopening of the works.

The Lowther Ironworks located on the north bank of the River Derwent, c.1921, viewed from the south. The disused and abandoned furnaces lie idle, whilst some production continues at the Oldside Ironworks in the distance. Oldside Ironworks finally ceased production in October 1930. In the foreground is the main railway line running north to Maryport, out of Workington's Low Station. Many of the townspeople who were employed at the works on Oldside crossed over the river to and from work using the wooden cantilevered walkway fixed to the west side of the railway bridge. At its northern end was a small hut where an attendant collected a halfpenny toll from each worker. The bridge later became affectionately known as Ha'penny Billy's bridge. (Helena Thompson Museum)

A decade later, the ironworks were seriously hit by the 1892 Durham miners' strike. This lasted many months and the shortage of coke virtually brought the plant to a standstill. Lowther Ironworks subsequently closed in February 1893. Three years later, it was reported in the local press that 'not a single blast furnace was in blast at any of the works' north of the River Derwent. The Oldside area, once the hub of the town's thriving iron and steel industry stood 'desolate and almost deserted'. In 1897, the ironworks changed hands once more and was acquired by the Lowther Haematite Iron & Steel Co. Production at the works eventually recommenced and by the turn of the century Bulmer tells us the works consisted of 'three large modern blast furnaces'. However, the minutes of the Cleator and Workington Junction Railway Co. reveal that it was 'at a standstill once more' by August 1901. Four years later, the Workington Iron Co., which also operated the old Workington Haematite Ironworks close by, acquired the Lowther Ironworks and production began yet again in September 1905. Following the 1909 amalgamation of the town's iron and steel plants, the Lowther works were eventually closed for the last time as the blast furnaces were considered outdated and obsolete.

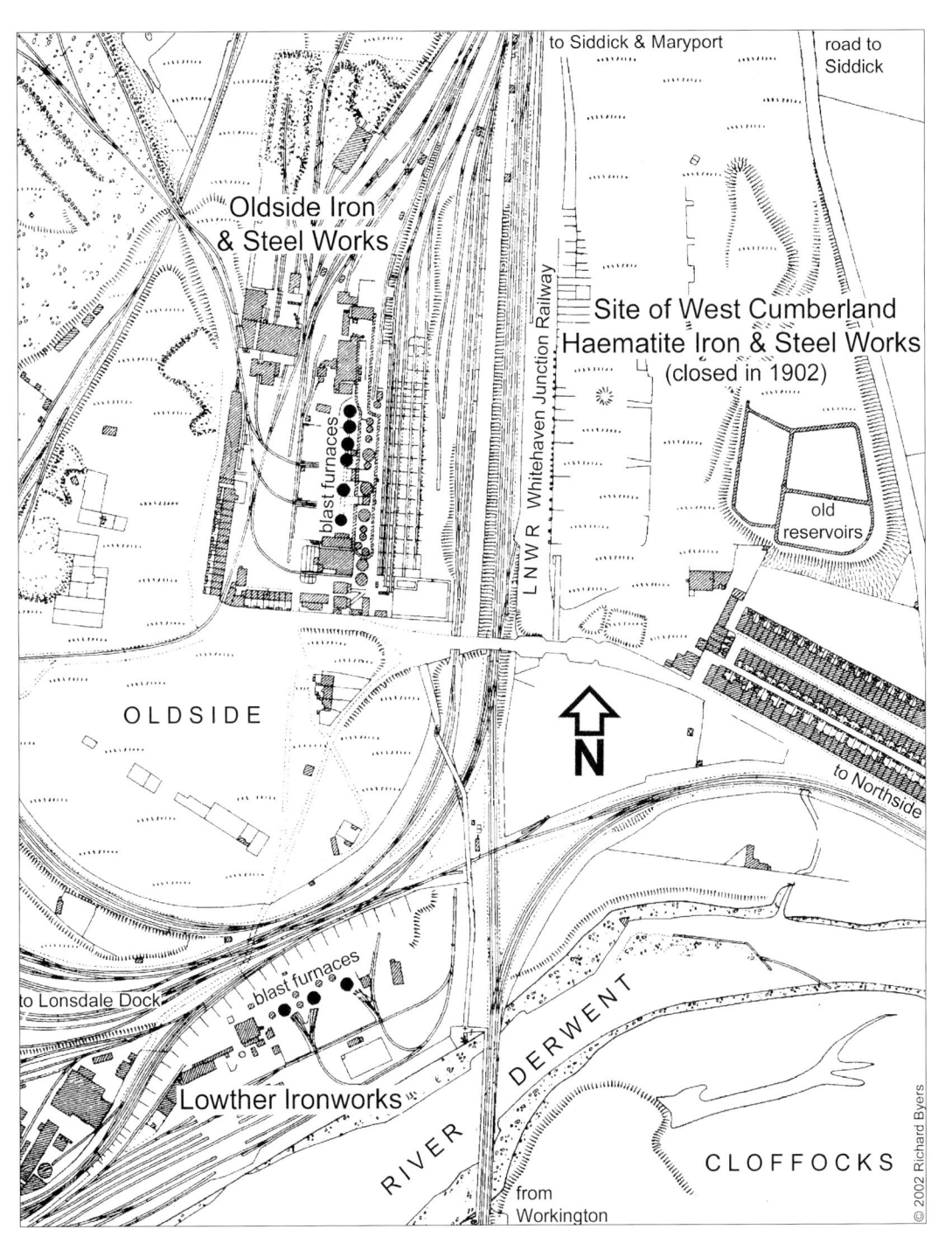

Another sketch map of the Lowther Ironworks based on the 1923 OS plan, showing its close proximity to the Workington Haematite Ironworks (later renamed the Oldside Iron & Steel Works) and the West Cumberland Iron & Steel Works. The photograph on the previous page was taken from the Cloffolks at the foot of this plan. A 1999 aerial photograph of the former Lowther Ironworks site, on the north bank of the River Derwent.

Almost ninety years have passed since the works closed, yet much of the red-brick retaining wall, with its distinctive buttresses, can still be seen today, running along the northern boundary of the works (see top of photograph). The main railway line out of Workington's Low Station runs from left to right north to Maryport. The Derwent Park rugby league and speedway stadium is in the centre of the photograph.

five

Moss Bay Haematite Iron Co.
Moss Bay Iron & Steel Co.

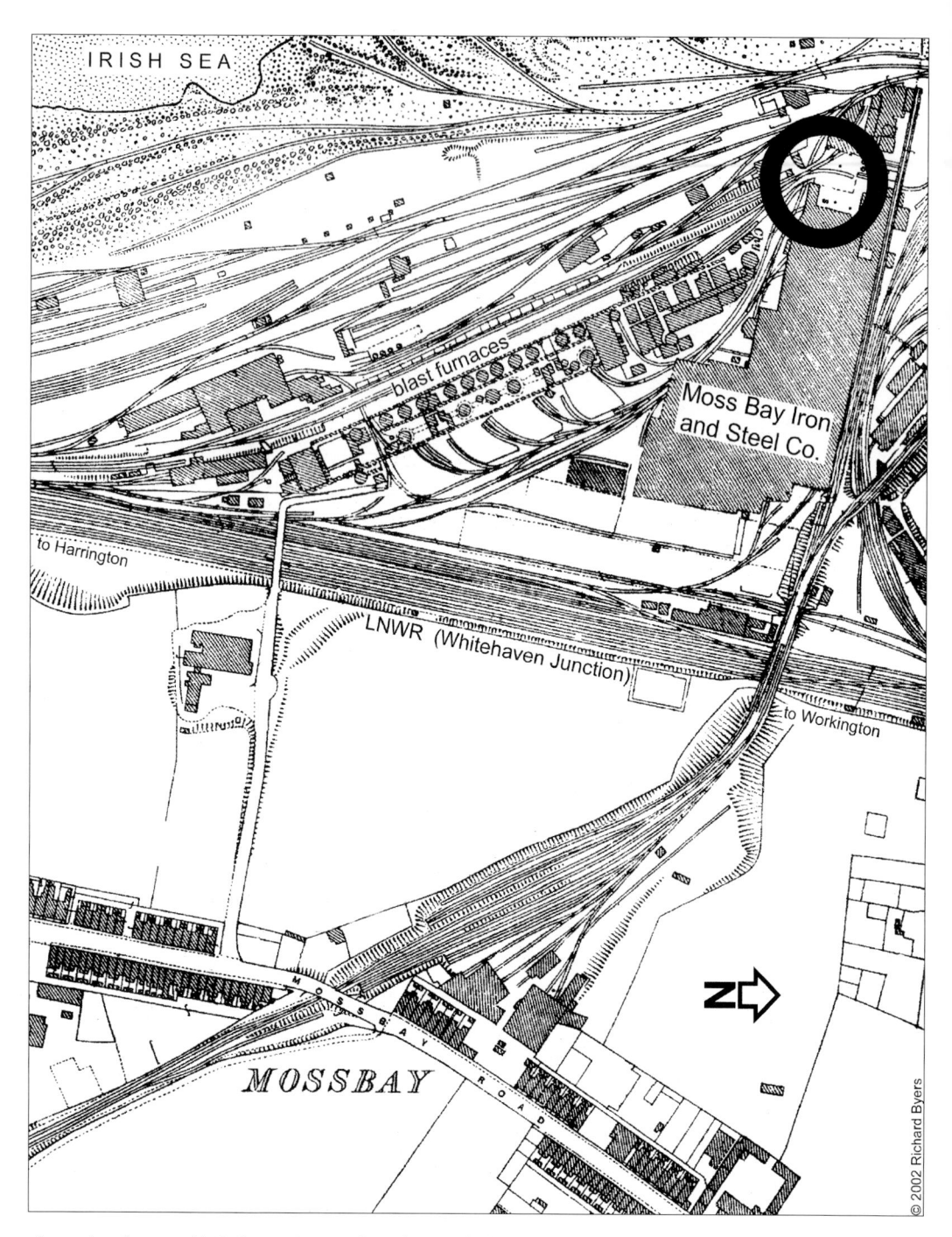

A map based on an old Ordnance Survey plan, showing the layout of the Moss Bay Iron & Steel Works in 1923. Today, the Moss Bay site, situated between the coast and the main railway line from Workington to Harrington, is occupied by Corus Rail. The area circled highlights the location of the Moss Bay Bessemer steel plant which operated here from 1877 to 1934. It is shown in more detail on the forthcoming pages.

The Moss Bay Ironworks was located at Moss Bay (or Westfield as it was often then called) to the south of Workington, between the coastline and the main railway line from Harrington into the town. The site is identified on the plan on p.6 by the letter D. The Moss Bay Haematite Iron Co., which operated the ironworks, was established in the early 1870s. From the Curwen archives, we learn that Henry Fraser Curwen leased the land to Peter Kirk, Charles James Valentine, Henry Kenyon and Mary Gibson on 24 July 1872. Charles J. Valentine (1837–1900) was the brother-in-law of Peter Kirk (1840–1916), having married his sister, Annie Kirk. Both men were already quite successful running the Quayside Forge, or Quayside Ironworks, in Stanley Street. Here production was limited to the manufacture of wrought iron in the puddling furnaces. Douglas R. Wattleworth, writing in 1965, believed that 'it was from the Quay Forge that the origins of the Moss Bay works can be traced'.

The Moss Bay Ironworks was originally erected to meet the growing demand for Bessemer pig iron, the basic raw material of steelmaking. The company then simply cast and sold the pigs, or blocks of iron, to steel plants up and down the country and abroad. But, by January 1876, they announced that they too were to 'add the manufacture of steel to their already extensive business'. The company adopted the relatively new process patented by William Deighton, whereby molten pig iron from the blast furnace was kept in a fluid state and transferred immediately to the Bessemer converter, thus saving the cost of heating and remelting the pig iron in a cupola or furnace. Three Bessemer converters of 8 tons' capacity and a new rail-rolling plant were constructed at Moss Bay, just north of the blast furnaces. This rolling mill was driven by another enormous steam engine, built by Miller and Anderson (of Coatbridge). Its massive flywheel measured 25ft in diameter and was said to weigh around 50 tons. In June 1877, the steel plant was completed and underwent trials, and two months later the first steel rail order was produced. In December 1879, the company was performing around twenty Bessemer blows per day.

In order to fund this growth and the cost of building the new steel plant, the Moss Bay company was converted into a new limited company in 1881. Both

Above: *Bankfield Mansion was built by Richard Schofield in 1876 for the local ironmasters, Peter Kirk and Charles James Valentine. This large, elegant property was essentially two semi-detached houses, with separate entrances at each end. It was located in its own extensive grounds, high above Banklands. Across the entire top floor was a single large room, used as a ballroom or function room on special occasions. It could be reached from either residence and was shared by both households.*

Left: *Peter Kirk (1840–1916), who, together with Charles James Valentine, established the Moss Bay Haematite Iron Co. in 1872. Both men later became joint managing directors of the Moss Bay Iron & Steel Co. in 1881. Kirk and his family emigrated to America in 1886, where he hoped to build a new modern iron and steel plant on the shores of Lake Washington. These plans never came to fruition and he retired to the San Juan Islands, where he died peacefully in 1916. (Michael Burridge Collection)*

Peter Kirk and Charles J. Valentine were appointed joint managing directors. It had a share capital of £350,000 and now traded as the Moss Bay Haematite Iron & Steel Co. Among its other first directors was another local businessman, Peter Gibson Quirk (1849–93). From 1882 to 1888, the chairman at the Moss Bay works was Joseph Ledger, formerly of the West Cumberland Haematite Iron Co.

In November 1884, Peter Kirk patented his design for the first steel railway sleeper and production was begun at Moss Bay. The Cleator and Workington Junction Railway Co. was amongst the first to use these innovative sleepers, intended to replace the conventional creosoted timber sleeper. In October 1885, they ordered 9,000 steel sleepers, paying 7s 6d each. These were required for the new line north of Workington's Central Station to Linefoot. It is very likely that the order was greatly influenced by Charles J. Valentine who was then a director of both Moss Bay and the railway company. Other larger orders are known to have been completed, including 160,000 steel sleepers, shipped from Workington to Bombay in India. Similar railway sleepers are still made at the Corus Rail's Moss Bay works today.

During the next decade Moss Bay continued to expand, although they were often trading at a loss or made only minimal profit. The company, which then employed over 2,000 men, also had to deal with significant industrial unrest, with several drawn-out strikes affecting production. For the first time, workers organised themselves into trade unions, as a defence against poor pay and harsh working conditions. Often, in difficult times when iron and steel prices were falling, the company would insist that its employees take a wage reduction. Naturally, a dispute between the ironmasters and their workmen was almost inevitable. The Moss Bay's workers had at their helm the socialist and union leader, Patrick Walls (1847–1932). A founder member of the Labour Party, he would also pioneer many improvements in working conditions. These ultimately benefited not just those at Moss Bay, but almost every worker at every ironworks throughout the country. Perhaps the major achievement of the tall Irishman, affectionately known as Paddy, was the establishment of a shorter working week. Previously his blast furnacemen had been forced to work an exhausting eighty-four hours a week. In 1890, Walls secured a new eight-hour daily shift system. Douglas R. Wattleworth told how 'he secured improved conditions through militant action, whilst steering his often unruly members along the path to peaceful negotiation and conciliation'.

In recognition of his service to the Trade Union movement, Patrick Walls later received an OBE. Between 1893 and 1931 he also served as a borough councillor, and became the town's first Labour mayor in 1915–16. He was eighty-four years old when he retired from public life in November 1931. Less than a year later, this remarkable man died at his home in St Michaels Road. Patrick Walls is buried alongside his wife Catherine in Harrington Road Cemetery.

The blast furnaces of the Moss Bay Ironworks, c.1895, viewed from the south east. The railway line from Whitehaven to Workington runs in a cutting across the foreground of the photograph. Each day hundreds of iron workers would pass back and forth across the footbridge on the left to and from their homes in Moss Bay. The blast furnaces and chimneys of the Derwent works can be seen in the distance.

The blast furnaces of the Moss Bay Ironworks viewed from the north east. This photograph was taken after the works were amalgamated into the new Workington Iron & Steel Co. in 1909. Thereafter, pig iron production was concentrated at the Derwent blast furnaces and there is little activity on the pig beds immediately in front of the blast furnaces. The Moss Bay soaking pits and rolling mill were located in the large building to the far right of the photograph. (Helena Thompson Museum)

In 1886, the Moss Bay managing director, Peter Kirk, left Workington and emigrated to America. He had become increasingly disillusioned by the day-to-day problems of the company and later wrote of the 'new and hopefully more prosperous opportunities' in the United States. Iron deposits had recently been discovered in the Cascade mountains of Washington State, and Kirk saw an ideal opportunity to build a modern iron and steel works on the shores of Lake Washington. This exciting venture was welcome relief for Kirk, away from the burden of running the troubled Moss Bay Co. Interestingly, the Lake Washington area of America was similar to West Cumbria, with coal and limestone resources (the essential elements of steel production) readily available in surrounding districts. He modelled much of his new plant on that at Workington, and even named it the Moss Bay Iron & Steel Works. The town around the proposed plant would also become known as Kirkland, named after its founder. Alan J. Stein, in his *History of Kirkland*, believed that Peter Kirk envisaged developing the area into the 'Pittsburgh of the West – a bustling new town whose economy would be focused around steel production'.

In reality, the success of his plans relied heavily on the building of a new ship canal through Seattle to the Puget Sound and a connection to the existing railroad system. But the Tacoma-based Northern Pacific Co. had control of this rail network and refused to allow a spur line to be built into Kirk's new works. Tacoma was in direct competition with Seattle, bidding to become the predominant seaport of Lake Washington. Consequently, they were reluctant to give Kirkland, and therefore Seattle, any great help or assistance. Surprisingly, Kirk seemed even more determined to see his dream project attain fruition. Along with prominent Seattle businessmen, he bought up thousands of acres of vacant land. Streets were laid out, and new houses were erected for the workers. Kirk also built Fir Grove, a new mansion for his large family. Today it is described as 'one of the finest homes in Kirkland'. His wife Mary Ann and their children left Bankfield to join him in July 1887.

The fatal blow to his dreams was the American stock market crash of 1893. Without a booming economy, no rail line would be built, no canal dredged, and no steel plant could survive. The works never opened and no iron and steel was ever smelted at Kirkland. Peter Kirk later retired to the island of San Juan, where he died in 1916. Today, Kirkland is a thriving city with a population of around 44,000 people. Peter Kirk's vision of a vibrant community on the eastern shore of Lake Washington has been fulfilled, although not exactly as he imagined it.

It is believed a number of Workington's inhabitants actually followed Kirk to seek employment in his new works. Certainly, his travels brought rail orders to Workington from that area of the United States. In 1886, 300 tons of T-section railway line were shipped from Workington for the Puget Sound Construction Co., which was then constructing the new Seattle, Lake Shore and Eastern Railway. John Boykin of Seattle revealed in 2002 that he possesses samples of these original '56lb per yard' rails, rescued from a scrap yard and bearing the old Moss Bay mill marks. Records confirm that there were also other batches of rails sent out to Seattle and Vancouver in British Columbia. We certainly know Charles Valentine visited Kirk in the United States in the summer of 1887, and Kirk is thought to have retained some shares and an interest in the Workington works for many years.

After Peter Kirk's departure, fortunes did not improve at the Moss Bay works. The company struggled on towards certain insolvency. Finally, a new company was formed to take over the bankrupt works and to continue production at Workington. Also named the Moss Bay Haematite Iron & Steel Co., it was incorporated in March 1891, with a share capital of nearly £310,000. Among its first directors were Charles James Valentine, John Scurrah Randles (1857–1945) and Robert Ernest Highton (1858–1931). Prior to his arrival in Workington, Highton had been employed as the London representative for the old Moss Bay Co. Highton was the son of a Keswick schoolmaster, the late Edward Highton. He had joined the Moss Bay works in 1881, after four years' employment as a clerk with the Cockermouth, Keswick and Penrith Railway Co. Within a decade, Highton rose to become the secretary and commercial

The upper level of the Moss Bay Bessemer shop in the early 1930s (see map on p.40). Within this area were three 16-ton capacity Bessemer converters arranged in a semi-circle. These were installed in 1912, replacing three smaller 8-ton capacity vessels. Ladles of molten pig iron were shunted up onto this raised area in order to fill or charge the Bessemer converters. With the aid of a hook on the hydraulic crane the ladle was titled and the molten pig iron was poured directly into the mouth of the converter. (Bessemer Steel Archive)

As the Bessemer crew remove fragments of skull or spillage which has solidified on the inverted centre vessel, a kibble or iron basket of cold scrap is dropped into the mouth of the far converter to reduce the temperature during the blow. In the foreground we can see the base of the other converter, which is also inverted. The base plate of each Bessemer converter was removable, in order to gain access to the tuyère box (or Holley bottom) which contained the tuyère plug. This plug was subject to rapid wear and erosion, and needed to be replaced after about thirty blows. (Bessemer Steel Archive)

manager of the new company. During its first year, several further improvements were undertaken at the Moss Bay works. Lancaster and Wattleworth tells that 'both the Bessemer department and the rail mill were able to report record outputs'. But the Durham miners' dispute, which had seriously affected output at the Lowther works, also brought production at Moss Bay to a halt. The Cumberland Union Bank withdrew its support and forced the Moss Bay Co. into liquidation once more. But the company appears to have successfully negotiated with its creditors and eventually traded through the problems.

During the first decade of the new century, with the worldwide market for iron and steel very much in decline, the Moss Bay works continued to struggle to make a respectable profit. In 1909, the Moss Bay Iron & Steel Co. were also amalgamated into the new Workington Iron & Steel Co. At the time of the transfer of ownership, the plant consisted primarily of four blast furnaces, three 8-ton capacity Bessemer converters, one open hearth furnace, a rail mill and fishplate mills. The Moss Bay board of directors still included Sir John Scurrah Randles and Robert Ernest Highton, together with William Burnyeat, Herbert Valentine, Joseph Ellis and F. Mallalieu.

Above: *A view from the lower level of the Moss Bay Bessemer shop looking west towards the three 16-ton capacity converters. In this area, the newly made steel was poured from the converter vessels into the teeming or casting ladle. With the aid of two hydraulic cranes moving in a series of interlocking arcs, the ladle of hot metal was moved across to the casting shop in the foreground. The other hydraulic crane in the distance is on the raised area shown in more detail in the previous photograph.* (Bessemer Steel Archive)

Opposite: *A sketch plan showing the basic layout of the Bessemer shop at Moss Bay, which operated from 1877 to 1934. The three Bessemer converters were located on the west side of the semicircular casting pit and are shown at the foot of the page. Ladles of molten pig iron to charge (or fill) the converters were shunted up the inclined rail track to the upper level (see p.46). Once a blow was completed, the molten steel was poured from the converter into a large teeming ladle supported on the transfer crane (see p.51). With the aid of the casting crane, the ladle was moved to above the casting pit area and the steel was poured off into individual ingot moulds (see p.52). After the steel had solidified, the ingots were stripped of their moulds and lifted into the soaking pits. All the cranes were hydraulically operated, and as mentioned above, moved in a series of interlocking curves or arcs in order that the ladles of hot metal and newly cast ingots could be easily transferred from one area to another.* (Bessemer Steel Archive)

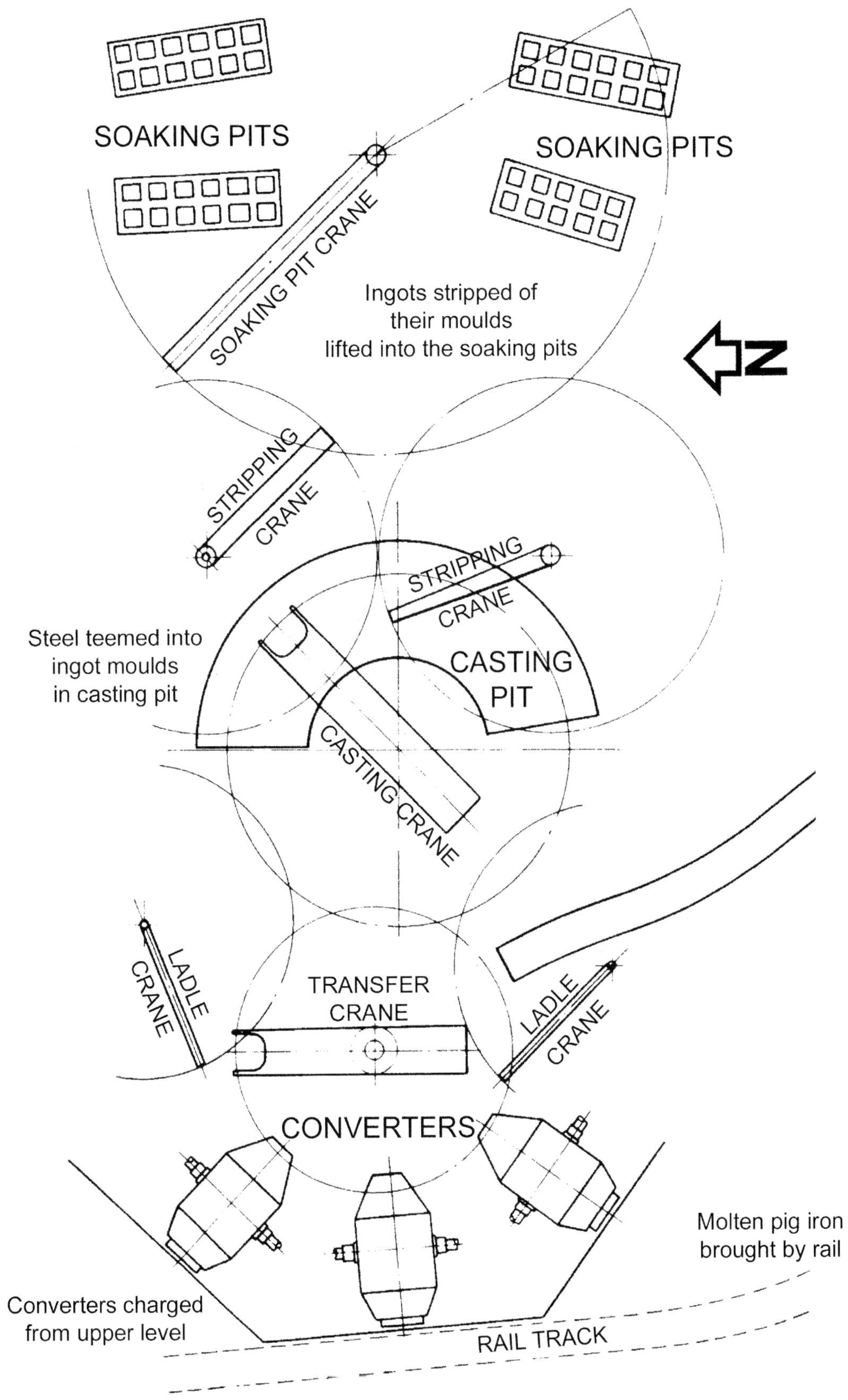
SOAKING PITS
SOAKING PITS
SOAKING PIT CRANE
Ingots stripped of
their moulds
lifted into the soaking pits
N
STRIPPING
CRANE
STRIPPING
CRANE
Steel teemed into
ingot moulds
in casting pit
CASTING
PIT
CASTING CRANE
LADLE
CRANE
TRANSFER
CRANE
LADLE
CRANE
CONVERTERS
Molten pig iron
brought by rail
Converters charged
from upper level
RAIL TRACK

One of the 16-ton capacity Bessemer converters at the Moss Bay steel plant during the final stage of a blow. A fierce white hot flame is observed from the mouth of the converter, as the carbon impurities are burnt out of the molten iron. The process, lasting less than twenty minutes, is almost complete and the pig iron in the vessel has been converted to steel. (Bessemer Steel Archive)

After a blow has been completed, the mouth of the converter is rotated downward. The molten steel is poured off into the teeming or casting ladle supported on the hydraulic transfer crane. This crane is then rotated in an arc and the ladle is passed to the casting crane. (See the plan of the Bessemer shop on p.49.) (Bessemer Steel Archive)

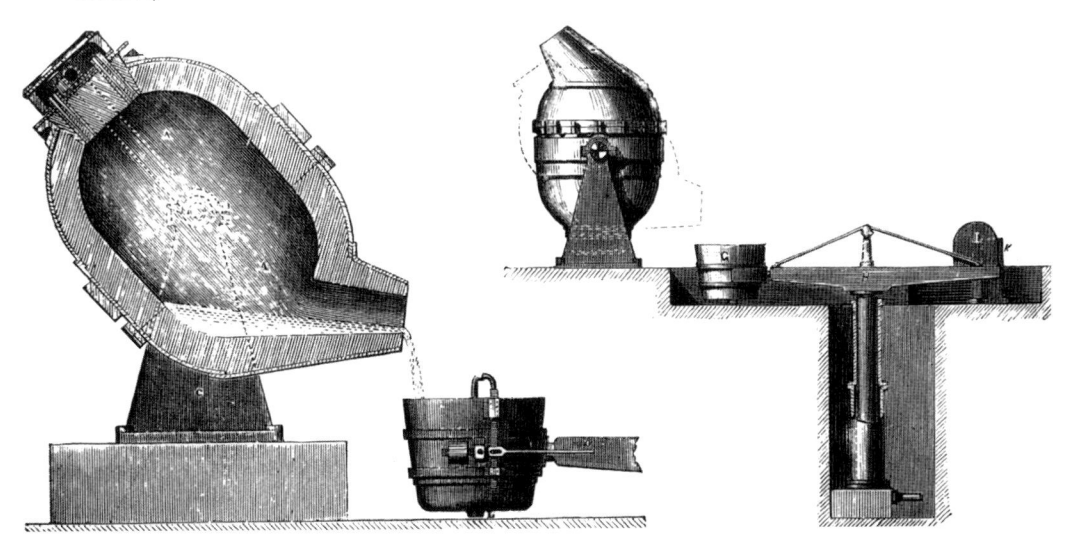

An old engraving (c.1892) showing a typical Bessemer converter, very similar to the 16-ton capacity vessels installed at Moss Bay in 1912. The illustration on the left shows a converter being emptied in much the same manner as the photograph above, whilst the engraving to the right shows the arrangement of the hydraulic transfer crane in more detail. Here the converter is vertical, the position adopted during a blow. Unlike the later vessels, these earlier models were rotated using hydraulic power.

Above: After the casting crane has moved the teeming ladle to the casting pit area of the Moss Bay Bessemer shop, the teemer fills a line of empty ingot moulds with newly made steel. This molten metal was poured through a valve in the base of the teeming ladle. This value was opened and closed by the teemer raising and lowering a handle on the outside of the ladle. Before the casting solidified, a pitman would place a cold steel loop into the molten steel. This allowed the ingot to be later stripped from its mould and transferred into and out of the soaking pits. (Bessemer Steel Archive)

Opposite above: Before the newly cast ingots could be successfully rolled, they had to be given a uniform temperature. This was achieved by lowering them individually into one of four coal-fired soaking pits. The white-hot ingots, or blooms as they were now known, were then transferred the short distance into the rolling mills. Here they were rolled back and forth through a series of rollers into railway lines or other steel sections. The above photograph shows the first stage of the rolling process, the cogging or breakdown mill. One bloom has undergone a few passes, whilst a second bloom is lifted into place. It is suspended on a hook and chain attached to the steel loop cast in place after teeming. (Bessemer Steel Archive)

Opposite below: The interior of the rolling mill at Moss Bay, c.1910. Three workers carry out some maintenace to the central mill (or stand) and appear to be removing the bottom roller.

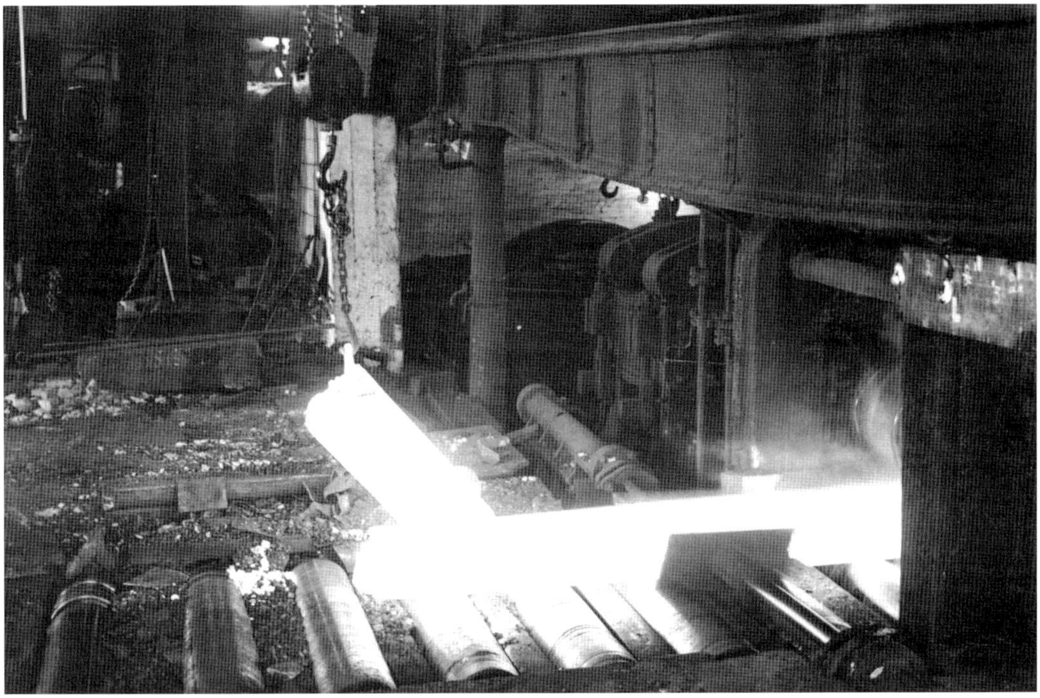

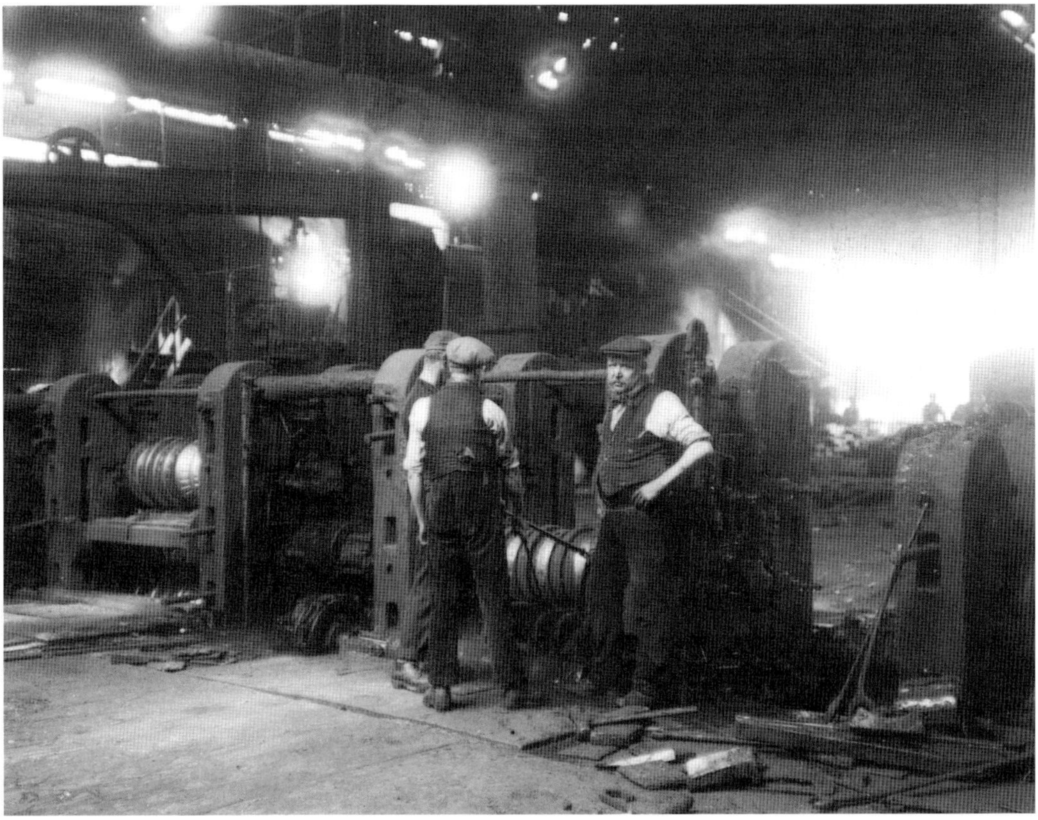

An interesting old engraving of the interior of Henry Bessemer's Steel Works at Sheffield, showing several similarities to the early steel plant at the Moss Bay Iron & Steel Works. In the foreground is an hydraulic crane supporting the teeming ladle over a semi-circular casting pit. The teemer carefully fills a line of empty ingot moulds, by operating the valve lever on the side of the teeming ladle. Unlike at Workington, where the converters were filled from a raised platform area, they were charged here with molten iron which was run down a chute directly into the mouth of the vessel. (Michael Burridge Collection)

six

New Yard Ironworks

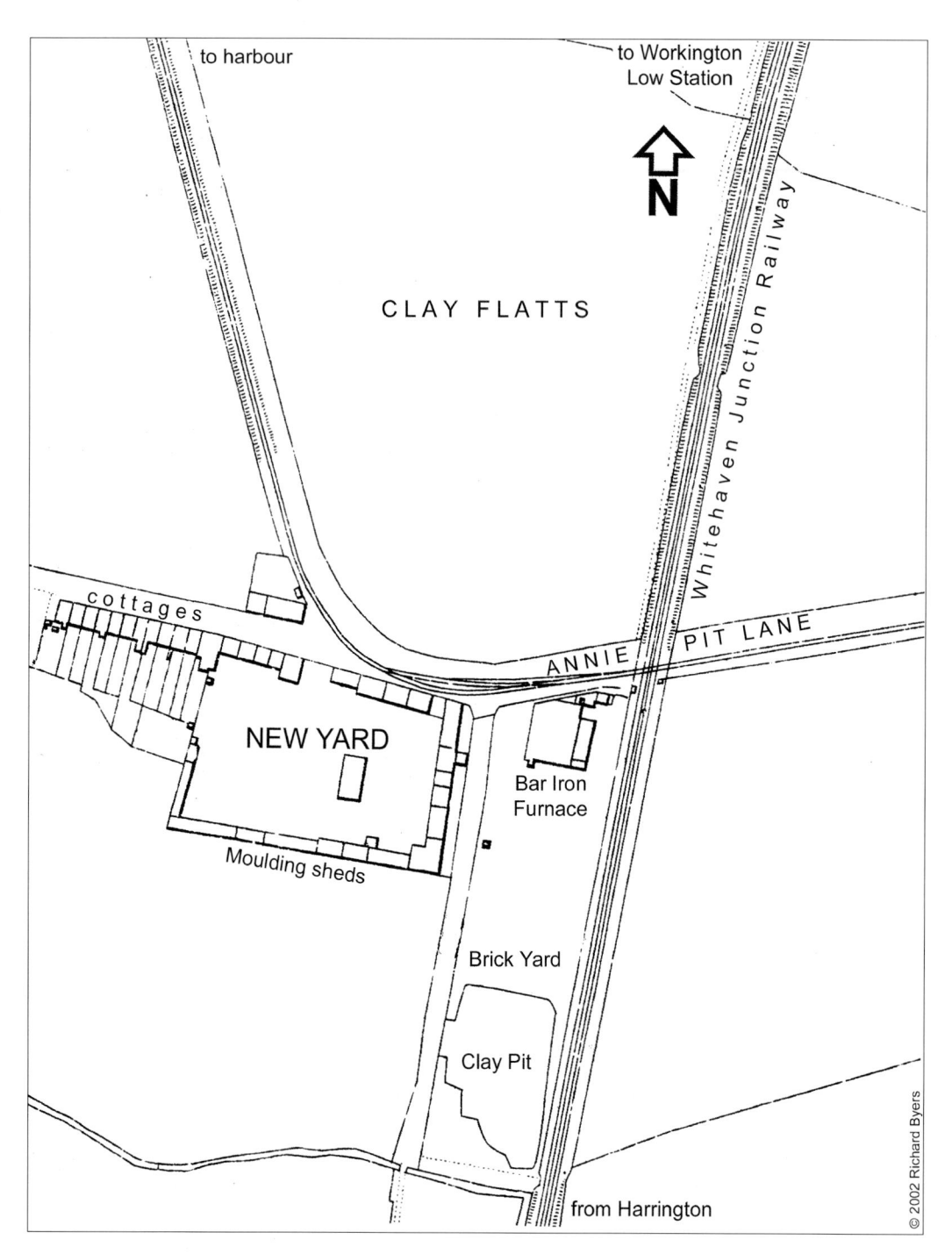

A sketch map of the New Yard Ironworks based on the 1863 OS plan. This plant was located close to where Annie Pit Lane passed over the Whitehaven Junction Railway, and started life as a foundry producing bar iron. New Yard had access to the harbour along the old waggonway which had originally been laid from Banklands and Moorbank collieries. This was also used by Jane and Annie pits and followed the line of Annie Pit Lane.

56

The New Yard Ironworks was situated just to the south of Annie Pit Lane, immediately west of the main railway line into Workington's Low Station. The Cammell & Co. steel plant was located to the south of this ironworks and actually encircled it on two sides. The site is identified on the location plan on p.6 by the letter G. New Yard was a relatively small ironworks in comparison to its larger neighbours and its very early history is something of a mystery. It certainly existed prior to the 1840s, as it appears on the plans of the proposed Whitehaven Junction Railway, prepared by the eminent engineer George Stephenson. We also know it started life as a simple iron foundry and was once probably operated by the Curwen family, perhaps in connection with their mining activities. Plans also show that around the perimeter of the works were built a number of small cottages which are thought to have housed the employees. In fact in those early days, New Yard seems to have existed as a small community, somewhat isolated from the rest of the town. Because of its close proximity to the ancient chapel of How Michael, it also seems to have been occasionally called Chapel Town.

During the 1860s, the Kirk family is thought to have acquired the foundry at New Yard. They also had an active interest in the the Quayside Forge (on Stanley Street) and would later also operate the Marshside Ironworks. Lancaster and Wattleworth tell us that the New Yard enterprise prospered and that new puddling furnaces and a rolling mill were installed at the works. At the beginning of 1880, work began on the construction of a blast furnace at the New Yard. Thought to have been built by the Workington Bridge and Boiler Co., it was sited at the rear of the moulding sheds. A large new steam engine was also installed to provide the powerful blast of air needed to smelt the pig iron. This was located in a new brick built engine house, beneath the tall chimney which can clearly be seen on several old photographs of the works that still exist today. Douglas R. Wattleworth, who started work in the town's iron and steel industry in 1907, vividly remembered the New Yard works around that time. He later recorded that 'the blast furnace was on the sea side of the public footpath that ran through the works, with the puddling furnaces etc. on

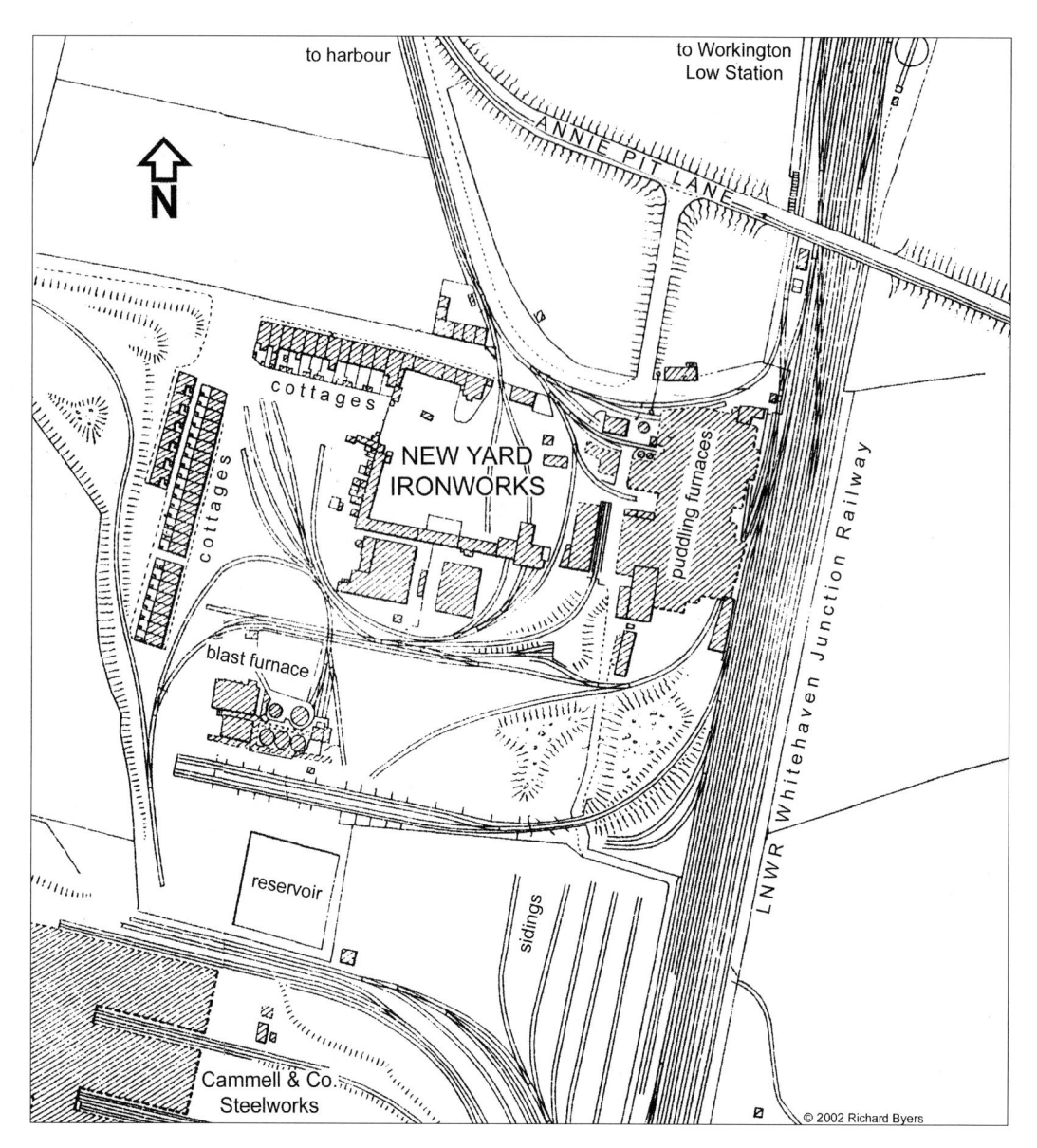

A sketch map of the much enlarged New Yard Ironworks based on the 1923 OS plan. The blast furnace and engine house situated at the rear of the moulding sheds were built in 1880. The molten iron smelted here was transferred by ladle directly to the pre-treatment furnace, prior to being charged into the puddling furnaces. These furnaces were located within the large building adjacent to the LNWR line from Harrington to Workington. Despite some alterations to the line of Annie Pit Lane, New Yard still appears to use the old waggonway to transport goods to the harbour. But in addition the plant now has a connection to the main railway line. Since the works were acquired by the Kirk family, around thirty additional terraced cottages for workers have been been erected along the western side of the site.

the other. Hot metal was taken by ladle to the pre-treatment furnace, before charging to the puddling furnaces.'

In February 1881, when the new blast furnace at the Kirks' New Yard works was first charged, there was a massive explosion which totally destroyed the top of the new structure. One newspaper report tells how the 'enormous boom' could be heard over the whole town. Thankfully no one was killed or injured in the explosion, and the blast furnace was rapidly repaired. It was finally commissioned and cast its first pig iron two weeks later. Despite having what was described as a 'plethora of orders', Kirk Bros found themselves on the brink of bankruptcy within just a few months, perhaps as a result of their huge expenditure at New Yard and their recent purchase of Ellen Rolling Mills at Maryport. But after continuing to trade during these difficult times, they eventually reached an agreement with their creditors and the liquidation was halted.

New Yard must have enjoyed some years of relative prosperity, as Bulmer records that its output in 1901 was about 25,000 tons of pig iron. But competing alongside the much larger iron producers in the town was fraught with difficulties. The Kirks remained in control until well past the turn of the century, employing about 350 men and boys. Then, as we know from Joseph Huntrods' biography, the works passed to 'Mr Morrison, one of the richest men in the country'. And it was he who first brought Huntrods to the town in an attempt to 'restore its fortunes', although this was described as 'an impossible task'. The New Yard works were eventually acquired by the Workington Iron & Steel Co. Much of the works site was cleared in the 1930s and the new coke oven plant was eventually erected there.

The Kirk family eventually also acquired the Marsh Side puddling furnaces and rolling mill, which was established by Dixon and Bayliss in 1869. The Marsh Side Ironworks was located between the rear of the properties on the south side of Stanley Street and at the back of the houses on Marshside, close to the south end of Marsh Street. Much of this area disappeared when the Marsh and Quay areas were cleared in the 1980s. Lancaster and Wattleworth tell us that in 1872, 'after a period of idleness', Marsh Side began trading as Price and Dixon. They also suggest that the works were presently undergoing some alterations and extensions. Exactly when it was acquired by the Kirk family is not clear, although when Henry Kirk read a paper entitled *Puddling in the Single Hand Furnaces* to the Iron and Steel Institute in September 1876, he is listed as 'proprietor of the New Yard and Marsh Side works'. In 1901, Bulmer tells us that Marshside Ironworks employed around 150 men and had one forge and a single rolling mill. He added that the combined annual output at this time (from both the New Yard and Marshside works) was 25,000 tons of bars and rivet iron, and from 650 to 1,000 tons of iron and brass castings. The Marsh Side works were still operating in 1907, as a factory inspector's report exists in the borough council's archives.

Bonnafoux's old engraving depicting the manufacture of steel by the Bessemer process, published c.1895. This layout was very similar to the Charles Cammell & Co. steel works at Workington. The 12-ton capacity converters were also arranged in pairs, facing each other and located under similar ventilation hoods (see p.62).

seven

Derwent Haematite Ironworks
Charles Cammell & Co. Ltd
Cammell Laird & Co. Ltd

Cammell Laird & Co. Steel Works, c.1900, viewed from the north. The chimneys of the Derwent blast furnaces can be seen in the distance. The Bessemer converters, soaking pits and rolling mills were located within the large building to the left. Steel rail and sleeper production ceased here in 1909 after the Cammell works were amalgamated within the new Workington Iron & Steel Co. (Helena Thompson Musuem)

The interior of the Bessemer steel plant at Charles Cammell & Co.'s Derwent works, c.1890. Unlike in the engraving on p.60, casting or teeming of the molten steel into the ingot moulds was not usually performed with such a small ladle. Between each pair of converters was a hydraulic crane, very similar to those at Moss Bay. It revolved over a circular casting pit, where the empty ingot moulds were placed ready for filling. (Michael Burridge Collection)

In November 1873, as the first pig iron was smelted at the Moss Bay plant, construction had already begun on another new ironworks in the town. The blast furnaces of the Derwent Haematite Iron Co. were built on the vacant land immediately to the north of Moss Bay works and just to the south of New Yard. The site is identified on the location plan on p.6 by the letter E. Again this new ironworks was established to meet the extraordinary demand for Bessemer pig iron. The majority of the investors in the new Derwent works appear to have been from the Kilmarnock area of Scotland. Newspaper reports record that its first blast furnace was 'blown in' during June of 1875. However, production was delayed for several months due to an unfortunate series of mechanical breakdowns. Despite the apparent recession elsewhere in the iron trade, the company began building a second blast furnace in March 1876, and added a third by 1880.

In July 1879, the directors of the Derwent Haematite Ironworks, now managed by Thomas Barbour (1827–96), are known to have approached Wilson Cammell and Co. (of Dronfield, near Sheffield) with a proposal that the two companies should merge. Austin & Ford, in their 1983 book *Steel Town*, tell us that 'the Dronfield works was, in terms of output and productivity, one of the foremost rail-producing plants in Britain, if not the world'. It appears that the Derwent works had regularly supplied Bessemer pig-iron to the Sheffield company, for conversion and rolling into rails. By September 1881, the local press in Yorkshire now confirmed that 'an arrangement had been made for the Dronfield steel works to be removed to Workington, where it will be placed beside the Derwent furnaces'.

Throughout the 1870s, many technological advances had occurred in Bessemer steelmaking. Primarily, it was now accepted that iron should now be transferred from the blast furnace direct to the converter in molten state. Dronfield had no blast furnaces, and it was over 120 miles from Cumberland's phosphorus-free iron ore reserves, then essential for the Bessemer steelmaking. The Derbyshire company also suffered geographically in other ways, as all export orders had first to be sent long distances by rail to the nearest port. The

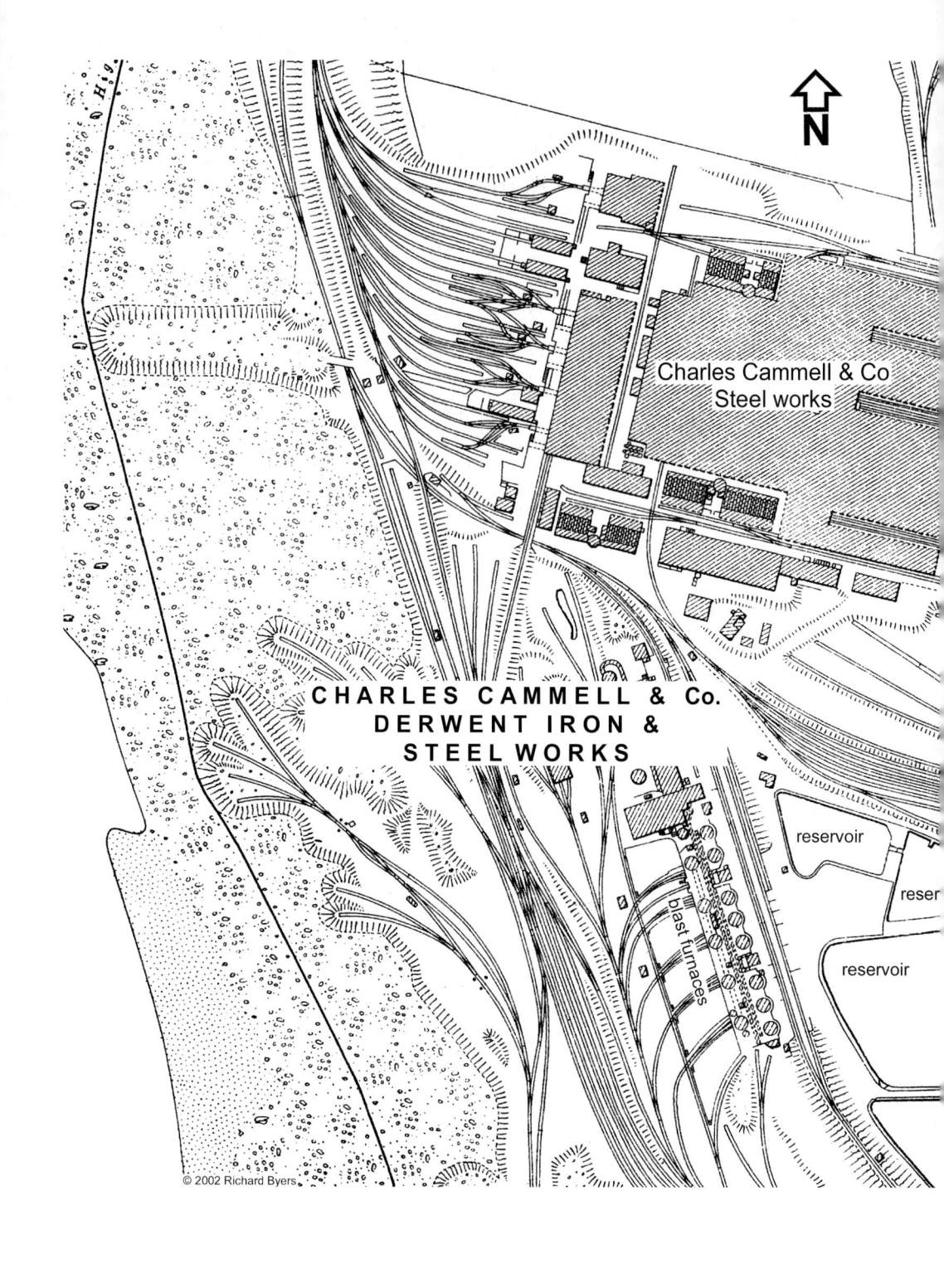

CHARLES CAMMELL & Co.
Steel works

**CHARLES CAMMELL & Co.
DERWENT IRON &
STEEL WORKS**

blast furnaces

reservoir

reser

reservoir

© 2002 Richard Byers

N

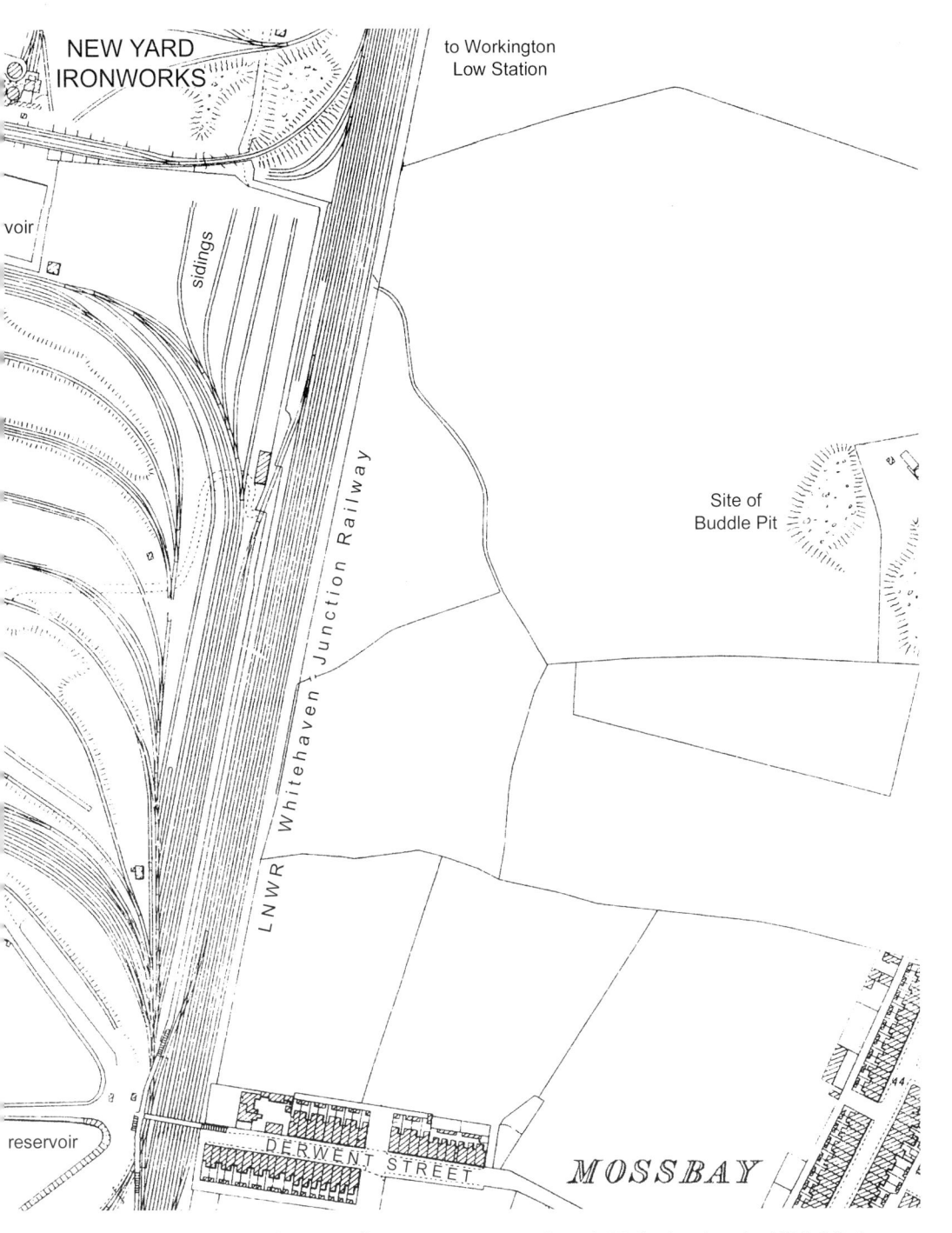

A sketch map of the Charles Cammell & Co. Derwent Iron & Steel Works, based on the 1923 OS plan. The steelworks erected in 1883 were located in the large building to the north of the blast furnaces and close to the southern boundary of the New Yard Ironworks.

The blast furnaces of the Derwent Ironworks in the 1950s, viewed from the east with the reservoirs in the foreground. Pig iron production began here in June 1875 and continued to be smelted on this site for another century. The three blast furnaces are located in the centre of the photograph, either side of which are the rows of tall regenerative stoves used to pre-heat the air blast. Each blast furnace was a different size, ranging from 15ft 9in (4.8m) to 20ft (6m) in diameter.

Another photograph of the Derwent blast furnaces in the 1950s, viewed from the north west. Unlike the earlier blast furnaces which were filled by hand from the gallery or platform at the top of each furnace, these three furnaces, then operated by the United Steel Companies, were mechanically charged and were capable of producing 8,600 tons of pig iron per week.

economic advantages of combining both plants at Workington were obvious. But this situation was not unique to Wilson Cammell; other Sheffield rail producers faced much the same problems. One such company was Charles Cammell & Co., which then ran the nearby Cylops and Penistone works. Despite trading independently, these two companies essentially belonged to the Cammell and Wilson families, as their respective names would suggest. They also shared several directors, many of whom were old and trusted friends. The two Sheffield companies then struck a happy compromise. Charles Cammell & Co. would now purchase both Wilson Cammell's Dronfield works and Workington's Derwent works. Dronfield would still close and transfer as planned, to the site north of the Derwent blast furnaces. The combined Workington plants would now be operated by Charles Cammell & Co., and would concentrate principally on export orders for steel rails.

Cammells purchased the Derwent Ironworks for £105,000; the whole amount was paid by the creation of £300,000-worth of additional share capital. They also acquired two adjacent fields belonging to Joseph Thompson. They now had a large site covering between 80 and 90 acres. By the summer of 1882, the £50,000 contract for building the new steel plant at Workington had been given to a local contractor, Richard Harrison Hodgson. William Tomlinson (of Dronfield) was appointed as clerk of works for the scheme.

Production ceased at the doomed Dronfield works on Saturday 1 March 1883. Newspaper reports recording the closure note that James Duffield (then manager of the Dronfield works) thanked his Dronfield workforce, amidst a sombre but 'good natured' ceremony, more reminiscent of a wake. As a genuine gesture of atonement, he said he would gladly offer jobs 'to any old hands' who planned to move north to Workington. The closure contributed to the significant decline of the Derbyshire town. By 1886, more than a third of the 934 houses in Dronfield were unoccupied, as upwards of 2,000 people left the town. Shop after shop in the main street was vacated and their windows boarded up. Dronfield, a once thriving industrial town, 'became known throughout the district as the deserted village'.

A considerable number of Dronfield's workmen were engaged to assist in the dismantling of their former workplace. Most of its machinery and plant was brought by rail to Workington, and re-erected at the Derwent Ironworks site. Another newspaper report tells us that Cammells even brought the 'tin sheeting roofs from Dronfield' to re-erect at Workington. A trusted Cammell engineer, Josiah Purser (1848–1928), oversaw this process and subsequently settled in the town. In the weeks and months following the Dronfield closure, many hundreds of his former workforce joined him, their arrival triggering the development of the Moss Bay area (formerly referred to simply as Westfield). The majority of its houses were built to accommodate the incoming steelworkers. Whilst the steelwork move had turned Dronfield into something of a ghost town, Workington became a boom town.

The 'Dronnies', as they became known, were initially greeted with some hostility by the local people. They were considered more skilled and often better paid, and their arrival *en masse* also resulted in higher rents and rising prices. It took some time for the two communities to become fully integrated. Whilst it is not easy to calculate the actual number who migrated to the town, it is suggested that in excess of 1,400 men, women and children made the journey north. It should be noted that less than 45 per cent of these were actually born in that area of Derbyshire (or neighbouring Sheffield). A significant number had simply migrated from elsewhere to the Dronfield works after it first opened in 1873. Now they moved once more to Workington in search of employment.

Under the watchful gaze of Messrs Wilson, Duffield, Bradbury and Oates, production at the new Derwent steel plant began in the autumn of 1883. Six 12-ton capacity Bessemer converters had been installed, arranged in three casting areas or pits. The first steel rails were rolled on Thursday 18 October, just six months since the machinery was last in motion at Dronfield. Records point to these first rails being supplied to the North Eastern Railway Co. Around this time, they also supplied 72,000 tons of steel rails to be shipped to New South Wales, and a further 2,000 tons to the Belgian Railway in Brussels. Other major orders soon followed from Argentina, Japan and India. The output from its three original Derwent blast furnaces was often inadequate to meet the demands of the new rail mill. Each was raised in height, to increase their capacity by about 30 per cent. Lancaster and Wattleworth reveal that it was still necessary for Cammells to buy in pig iron from elsewhere. This was converted to steel and rolled into more rails, in order to fulfil their backlog of orders. To remedy this shortfall two additional blast furnaces were erected at the Derwent works by the winter of 1898.

In October 1903, Cammells merged with Laird Brothers Ltd and thereafter traded as Cammell Laird and Co. A year later they purchased the town's Lonsdale Dock. This was an obvious move, for in the 1880s, vast iron ore deposits had been discovered in Spain and North Africa. Large quantities of this cheaper and far richer foreign ore were now being shipped to the UK. Cammells felt that gaining control of Workington port was both essential and cost effective. Unfortunately, these imports of cheaper foreign iron ore eventually brought about the demise of the West Cumberland haematite mines.

In 1909, the Cammell Laird Iron & Steel Works in the town and its other Cumberland properties, which included the Solway Ironworks at Maryport and three iron ore mines at Frizington and Bigrigg, were amalgamated into the new Workington Iron & Steel Co. At the time of the transfer, Cammell's plant at Workington consisted primarily of five blast furnaces, eight Bessemer converters, one open hearth furnace and rail, tin bar and fishplate mills.

eight

Workington Iron & Steel Co. United Steel Companies

Left: *The Borough of Workington municipal coat of arms between 1881 and 1950. Workington is justifiably proud of its iron and steel heritage and this is reflected in the town's first coat of arms. Records suggest it was designed by John Snowdon Armstrong who lived in Fisher Street. He is thought to have copied the blast furnace from those at Oldside.*

Right: *The Borough of Workington municipal coat of arms between 1950 and 1974. When the town commissioned a new coat of arms, the figure of Vulcan, the Roman god of metal workers, was included to depict once again the town's rich iron and steel history.*

pp.72-3: *Aerial photograph of the Workington Iron and Steel plant, c.1952, viewed from the south west. To the bottom right is the Moss Bay steel plant, which incorporated the Bessemer shop, soaking pits and rolling mills. In the centre of the photograph are the Derwent blast furnaces. The coke ovens were located a little further north, and extended over part of the former New Yard Ironworks site. Directly opposite, across the Harrington to Workington railway line, was the Solway Colliery. The winding gear of its pitheads can be seen in the top right-hand corner of the photograph. (Michael Burridge Collection)*

From the writings of Patrick Walls, we learn that during the first decade of the new century it was feared that iron and steelmaking in Workington 'would be crushed out as a result of the severe competition exerted by the large steel combinations of the United States, and the powerfully organised and state-aided works in Germany'. To alleviate these problems, the Workington Iron & Steel Co. Ltd was created in August 1909. This new company, with a share capital of almost £2 million, was formed by a fusion of the Moss Bay Haematite Iron & Steel Co., the Workington Iron Co., Cammell Laird's Cumberland properties and the Harrington Iron & Coal Co. There is some dispute as to who initiated the proposal to amalgamate; some imply it was Sir John Scurrah Randles (the town's MP), others suggest the it was board of Cammell Laird. Despite this confusion, it is clear that all the local companies eventually saw the real logic and mutual advantages of combining all their activities. Previously, despite their close proximity, each of the town's ironworks had traded relatively independently of each other. Local competition between the neighbouring companies would now be eliminated and their joint management would cut overall costs and secure the future of the industry in the town.

A contemporary newspaper report tells us the new company (often referred to as the 'combine') now boasted twenty-two blast furnaces, eleven Bessemer converters, two open hearth furnaces, six iron ore mines, a number of collieries and even a 'valuable manganese mine' in Mysore, India. They also effectively controlled both Workington and Harrington harbours. Sir John Randles was appointed the first chairman and the board of directors included Joseph Ellis, Herbert Valentine, W. Burnyeat, R.E. Highton and H.E. Wilson. Joseph Ellis and Herbert Valentine were the brother-in-law and son of the late ironmaster, Charles James Valentine.

One of their first decisions was to cease rail and steel sleeper production at the former Cammell Laird Derwent plant. This would now be concentrated only at the Moss Bay part of the new combind works. A new tyre and steel mill was then established at the old Derwent rail mill. Although the early years of the new company were still not very productive, they did achieve a more efficient

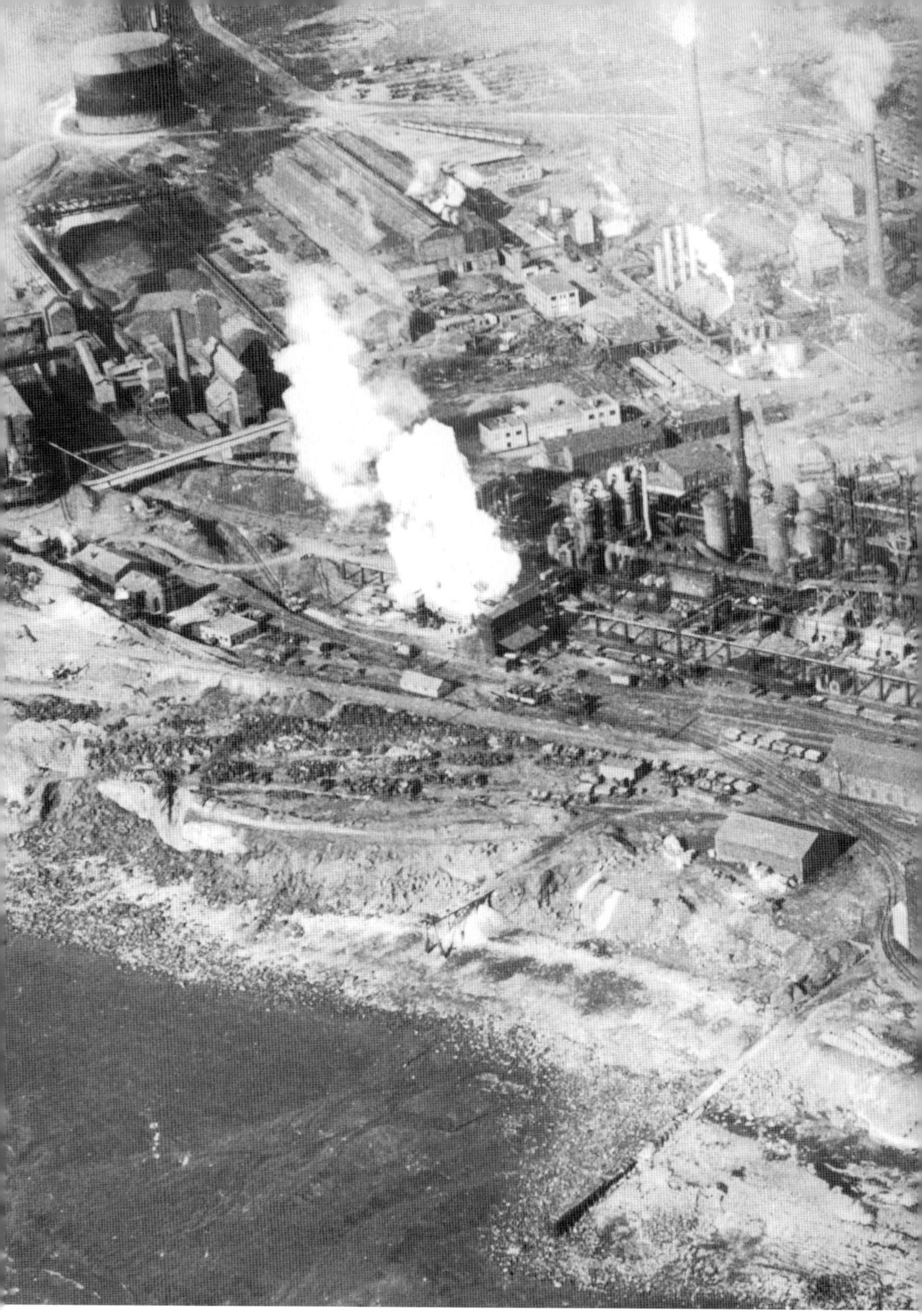

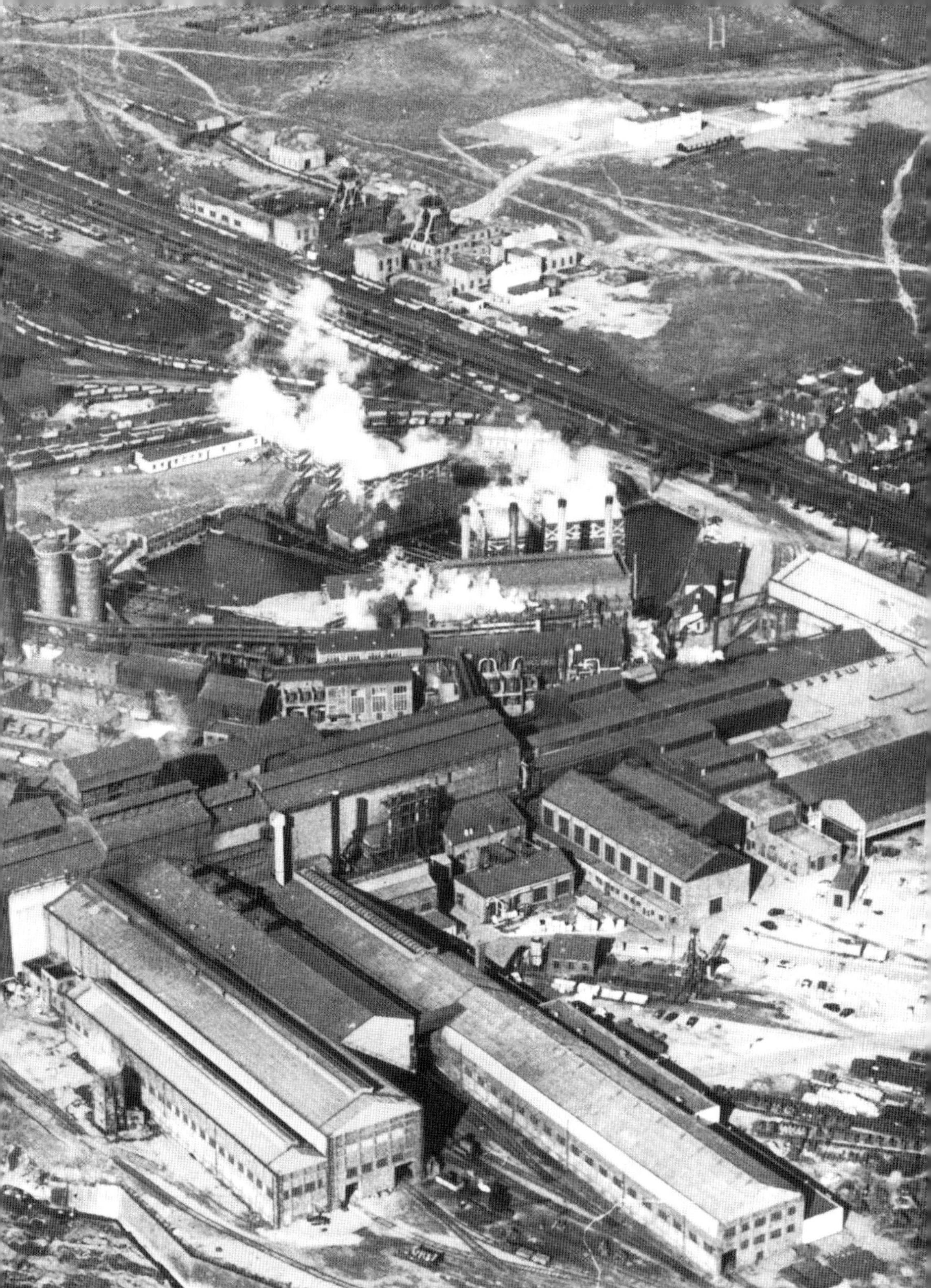

Invited guests gather on the specially erected stands to witness the visit of King George V and Queen Mary to the Workington Iron and Steel plant in May 1917. The blast furnaces of the Moss Bay works can be seen in the background. During these war years, George V was seen as very much as 'the people's king', making frequent trips to the battlefields of France. At home, his morale-boosting visits to important munitions plants such as Moss Bay were to encourage 'hearts and hands of the workers playing a different, but yet equally vital part' in the bitter conflict.

King George V, dressed in his khaki military uniform, was escorted around the plant by the works manager, Thomas W. Graham (left), and Joseph Valentine Ellis (right). Queen Mary was accompanied by the town's MP, Sir John Randles. During the visit the royal party were shown a blast furnace being tapped and watched the molten iron flow into the pig beds. They also witnessed a Bessemer blow, the King commenting that this magnificent spectacle was 'one of the best things he had seen that day'.

output of 13,000 tons of pig iron per week. This was in spite of the General Strike of September 1911, when it was said the company suffered 'paralysing stoppages', with all their blast furnaces being damped down.

In the early years of the First World War, Workington (and the nation generally) was slow to adapt iron and steel production for the war effort. It was not until after Lloyd George established the Ministry of Munitions in May 1915 that the industry was truly mobilised. All production (and prices) were subsequently controlled by the Government. Workington was not an established munition works, but by the summer of 1915 the works began manufacturing large quantities of shell steel. As more than 800 iron- and steelworkers had volunteered for military service, the town's women were rapidly trained to replaced them. The news of horrific losses due to shell shortages had only recently been made public. The outcry brought an immense increase in these women volunteers and bolstered their commitment to the cause. In order to accommodate these female workers in the previously male preserve, essential work had to be swiftly carried out at the plant. Conditions left a great deal to be desired, particularly the very primitive toilet facilities, which were totally inappropriate. H.B. Williams, the Borough Engineer, inspected the steelworks around this time and wrote: 'At one toilet near the shore was a simple low beam on which the men would roost; there were no divisions to form separate compartments, hence no privacy. The excrement was simply carried out to sea by the action of the waves.' During this period, despite the government restrictions and the change of workforce, production and profits became exceptionally high.

On 17 May 1917, King George V and Queen Mary paid a morale-boosting visit to Workington's iron and steel plant. After spending the morning in Barrow, the Royal Train arrived at Workington's Low Station at 3.15 p.m. It was met by Lord Lonsdale, then Lord Lieutenant of Cumberland, and Sir John Scurrah Randles MP. They travelled by royal car to the works, via Station Road, Oxford Street, down John Street and along Harrington Road. The King, wearing his khaki military uniform, was then escorted around the plant by Thomas W. Graham (works manager) and Joseph Valentine Ellis, whilst Sir John Randles accompanied Queen Mary during the tour. They were shown a blast furnace being tapped and watched the molten iron flowing into the pig beds. They witnessed a Bessemer blow, the King commenting that the magnificent spectacle was 'one of the best things he had seen that day'. From there they moved to the cogging and finishing mills, the acid open hearth furnaces, fish mill and power house. During their visit, the Royal Party was also introduced to Patrick Walls (of the Blast-furnace Men's Union), Thomas Cape (Cumberland Coal Miners' Association), T. Gavin Duffy (Cumberland Iron Ore Miners' Association) and William Cowan (Cumberland Quarrymen's Association). A few days later, a letter sent from the Royal Train to the town's mayor read: 'The King and Queen were very pleased with the warm reception accorded them at Workington.'

Right: *Sir John Scurrah Randles (1857–1945), who lived at Stilecroft House on Stainburn Road, was the first chairman of the Workington Iron & Steel Co., having previously served as a director of both the Workington Iron Co. and the Moss Bay Haematite Iron & Steel Co. In addition, he was also actively involved in the management of several local railway companies, serving as a director of the C&WJR, the FR and the CK&PR. In 1900–10, 1912–18 and 1919–22, Randles was the Conservative MP for the Cockermouth constituency, which then included Workington. He was also a member of Cumberland County Council. Knighted in 1905, he was made a freeman of the Borough of Workington in July 1916 in recognition of his services to the town's iron and steel industry.*

Below: *The Workington Munition Girls' Football Club, photographed at Lonsdale Park in 1917. During the First World War, the town's steel works was converted to manufacture large quantities of shell steel. As upwards of 800 employees had enlisted for military service, the town's women were rapidly trained to replace their menfolk at the works. Regular football matches were arranged to both raise funds for the war effort and boost morale. Interestingly, with the exception of the goalkeeper, this ladies' team seems to have played their matches wearing their everyday work clothes, consisting of a long smock dress, tied high at the waist, and large mop cap. (Joyce Byers Collection)*

In 1919, the Workington Iron & Steel Co. was taken over by the rapidly expanding United Steel Group. This Sheffield-based company had its origins in the nucleus of Steel, Peech and Tozer (of Rotherham) and Samuel Fox (of Stocksbridge) in 1917. Further acquisitions in Scunthorpe and Appleby (Lincolnshire) took place in the following year. Thereafter it was restructured into a limited company, and traded as United Steel Companies Ltd. The purchase of the Workington plant essentially guaranteed supplies of haematite pig iron to the Sheffield works. Initially, there was considerable overlap of production, as the various parts of United Steel had previously traded independently. It was not until the 1930s that any major rationalisation of production took place, and this was not fully implemented until after the Second World War. The manufacture of railway lines and associated products within the group was concentrated at Workington, together with the haematite and blast furnace ferro-alloys trades.

The end of the First World War was greeted by everyone with enormous relief and expectancy. But after a very brief and hectic boom, a catastrophic slump followed, which lasted many years. In 1920–21, UK steel production fell by over 55 per cent. This reduction was attributed to the major coal strike, and seriously affected the town's iron and steel works. Almost six months' production was lost, when the workers were laid off and the plant stood idle. Many the town's iron- and steel-workers were once again jobless, their families hungry and destitute. This serious recession now eclipsed in gravity the acute depression of the mid-1890s.

The 1963 steelmaking notes of Mike Burridge tell us that the period 1930–39 saw 'physical re-equipment, ordered price structures and technical progress in the steel industry' which led to something of a revival. By 1932, United Steel replaced one of Moss Bay's older blast furnaces with a modern unit, complete with skip-loading equipment. The remaining two blast furnaces were also later rebuilt, and provided with bucket-type chargers. Two years later, a new Bessemer steel plant comprising of two 25-ton capacity converters with a 400-ton hot metal mixer was commissioned. This replaced the three 16-ton converters which had been installed in 1912. A new steel ingot-casting shop, with a capacity of sixty-four 3-ton ingots, and two new soaking pits were also erected. In addition, a double-stand pig-iron casting machine was brought into use in 1936, and thereafter all sand casting ceased.

That same year, a new coke oven plant was also erected to the north of the Derwent blast furnaces. Built by the Woodhall-Duckham Co., it had fifty-three individual ovens. By 1940, a further eleven were added, bringing the company's weekly blast furnace coke production to 7,000 tons. Mike Burridge commented: 'Workington now possessed one of the most modern steel-making plants in Europe, if not the world.' As production almost trebled during this decade, the recovery stood the Workington works in good stead for the difficult war years that followed.

Pig iron is tapped from the foot of one of the Derwent blast furnaces into a 50-ton capacity ladle, supported on a rail bogie, c.1959. From here the ladle of molten metal was shunted by rail to either to the Bessemer shop to be converted into steel or taken to the pig caster (see pp.110-13).

Much of this work had been carried out under the guidance of Workington's general manager Thomas Whitley Graham. He had spent a lifetime in the iron and steel industry, gaining vast experience. At the age of fifteen, the youthful Graham had started his working life at the Derwent blast furnaces, working under Mr Paterson. In 1907, Graham first took over as manager of the Moss Bay furnaces, before becoming the manager of the entire works two years later. After the merger of the Workington iron and steel plants, he subsequently became manager of the 'combine'. A decade later he was appointed general manager of the Workington branch of the United Steel Companies. In 1938, the Workington Iron & Steel Company name was revived when United Steel converted its Cumberland branch into a new subsidiary company. Although now administered by a local board based in Workington, the parent company still retained the assets and overall general control.

Despite all the lessons learnt during the First World War, on the outbreak of war in 1939 the country was again relatively slow to increase its munitions manufacture. It was the shock of Dunkirk in May 1940 that awakened the nation and prompted Winston Churchill to swiftly address the situation. Very similar wartime controls and restrictions were once again imposed, essentially almost nationalising the industry. But several changes and developments in armaments now posed a major problem. During the first war, munitions were manufactured predominantly from cast iron and mild steel, but special heat-treated steels were now required. Early in the war, the German Army invaded Norway and essentially cut off the UK's supply of these essential special steels, such as alloy and stainless steel. Although for a short time some supplies were shipped across the Atlantic from America, it was soon clear that further electric-arc furnace steel plants had to be built in this country. Workington was chosen as one location for such a new plant, because of its isolated location away from the enemy. By February 1942, a new 20-ton furnace had been installed at Moss Bay whilst an additional one was commissioned at the new Chapel Bank works by the summer of 1943. Here four others were also later installed, although the last one is thought not to have been commissioned during the war years.

Work began on the construction of the Chapel Bank works in February 1941. Also known then as the 'Workington Shore works', they were formally opened by W.T.V. Harmer (of the Ministry of Supply) in October 1941. The plant was entirely funded by this government agency. Located on a 43-acre site below the shore hills, between the south bank of the River Derwent estuary and the blast furnaces of the Derwent works, it is still in production today. The site is identified on the location plan on p.6 by the letter F. Although presently part of Corus Engineering, over the years it has been known by a succession of different names. It started life during those early war years as the Distington Haematite Iron Co.; it was given this name to confuse the enemy as to its location and true purpose. This company name did still exist, but was inactive and had previously been associated with the blast furnaces at Distington on the

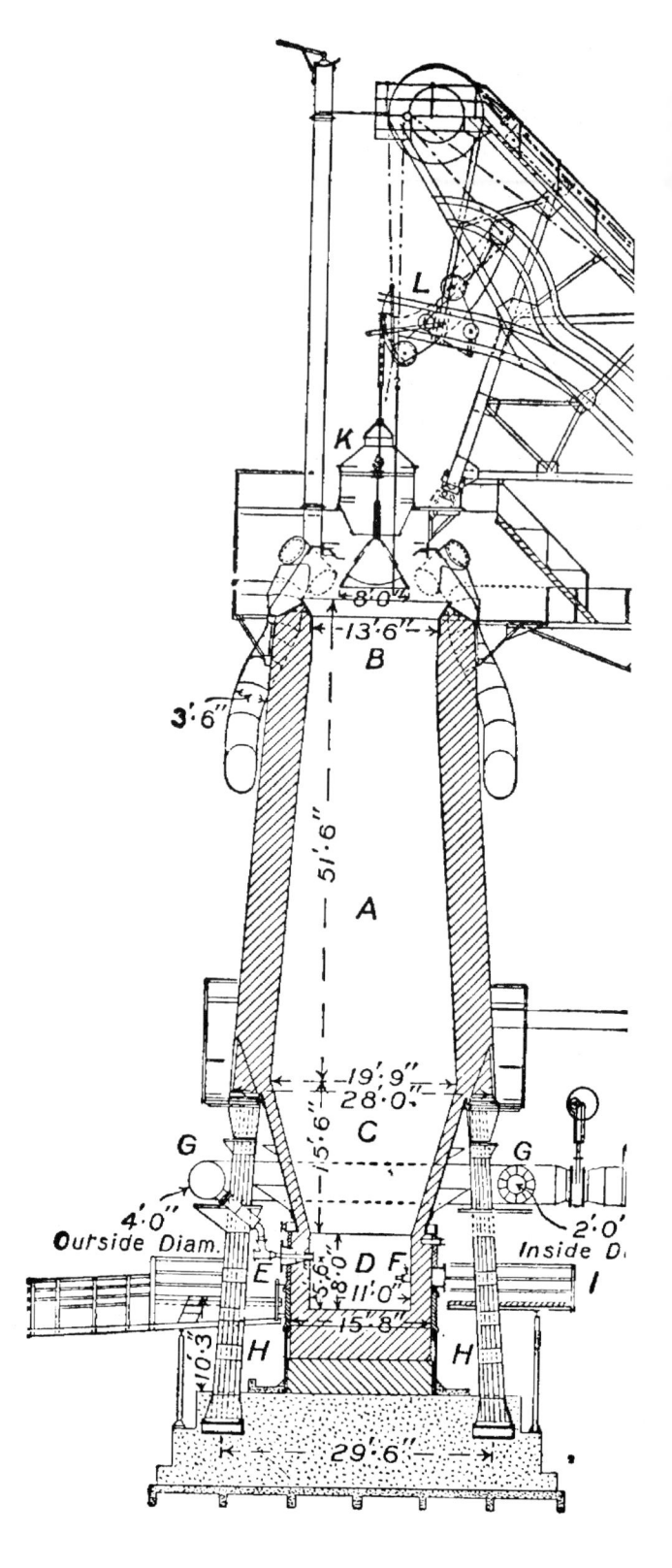

Vertical section through a modern blast furnace, typical of those at United Steel's Derwent Ironworks. The earlier furnaces were only capable of making around 600 tons of pig iron per week, but a modern furnace could smelt upwards of 2,000 tons. Apart from the increased capacity, the other principal improvements were the water-cooling of the walls and bosches to preserve the refractory lining, the more efficient supply and distribution of the blast, the disposal of slag and the modifications to the charging apparatus. (A) Stack, (B) throat, (C) bosches, (D) hearth, (E) blast main blowpipe and tuyères, (F) slag notch, (G) horseshoe main, (H) supporting columns, (I) platform, (K) charging bucket, (L) carriage. (Michael Burridge Collection)

outskirts of the town. As well as baffling wartime German intelligence, in more recent years it has also confused several local historians who still believe the new electric-arc furnace was actually built at Distington, not at Chapel Bank. Lancaster and Wattleworth confirm this by telling us that 'the only connection with Distington were the ornamental and imposing gates at the entrance to the works', which were said to have once 'graced the entrance to Distington Hall'.

The Chapel Bank works, named after their close proximity to the remains of the ancient chapel on the shoreline, was said to be the largest electric steel plant in the country. But after the war the plant were suddenly closed in December 1944. The redundant works were subsequently purchased from the government by United Steel Companies and operated thereafter by the newly formed Distington Engineering Co. The Chapel Bank works were converted into a modern foundry, largely specialising in the manufacture of haematite iron castings. The old furnaces were stripped out and the latest new machinery installed, comprising an engineering works, machine shops, press shop, and fabrication shop for platework and large, heavy items. Much of its early foundry work was the manufacture of ingot moulds and converter bottom plates used in steelmaking. The works also produced specialist mining equipment for Goodmans of Chicago, most of it being shipped out of Workington harbour. The company also became the sole manufacturer of tunnellers, duckbill loaders, ropebelt conveyors and shaker conveyors. By the 1960s, Chapel Bank housed the largest iron foundry in Europe, employing around 300 men, and was capable of producing about 2,000 tons of finished castings each week.

At the end of the Second World War, the British Government implemented controls to restrict the expansion of the steel industry. There were still difficulties in obtaining supplies, and shortage of particular steel products persisted long into the post-war period. Despite this, David Murray tells us that the British steel industry emerged from the war as a very 'strong going concern ... lean, battle scarred, but fighting fit'. The 1946 White Paper on the iron and steel industry proposed that Workington should principally concentrate its efforts on heavy steel rail production. This was an extremely logical suggestion in view of the modernisation work carried out at the plant during the previous decade or so. The Moss Bay works now covered 500–1,000 acres and was the sixth largest in the country by area.

By 1949, a new rail-finishing mill was installed at Workington and the old cogging mill at Moss Bay was completely replaced. This new 36-inch cogging mill rolled its first ingots in August of that year. Around six months later, a new turbo-blower with a capacity of 30,000 cubic feet per minute was installed to provide a more efficient blow to the two 25-ton Bessemer converters.

Workington was the only surviving bulk production acid Bessemer steel plant in Britain by the 1950s. Moss Bay now possessed three mechanically charged blast furnaces, having a gross output of 8,600 tons per week. The blast furnace plant located on the site of the old Derwent Ironworks had been completely

Tapping the base of one of the Derwent blast furnaces with an oxygen lance, c.1950.

rebuilt and modernised. A second new cogging or rolling mill with electric drive and a capacity of around 8000 tons per week was also installed. The majority of the old mill buildings were replaced and the remainder modernised.

In February 1951, the ninety-four main companies that made up the UK's iron and steel industry were nationalised by the Labour government. But, quite suprisingly, the industry was quickly returned to private ownership, in October 1952, following the Conservative general election victory. The United Steel Companies (still one of the largest companies) reappeared in much the same form as their pre-nationalised counterpart. Many believed an opportunity to reconstruct the industry in a positive way was lost with this denationalisation. It would be a further fifteen years before the Labour government got the opportunity to nationalise the industry once more. On 28 July 1967, the Workington Iron & Steel Co. was absorbed into the newly created British Steel Corporation.

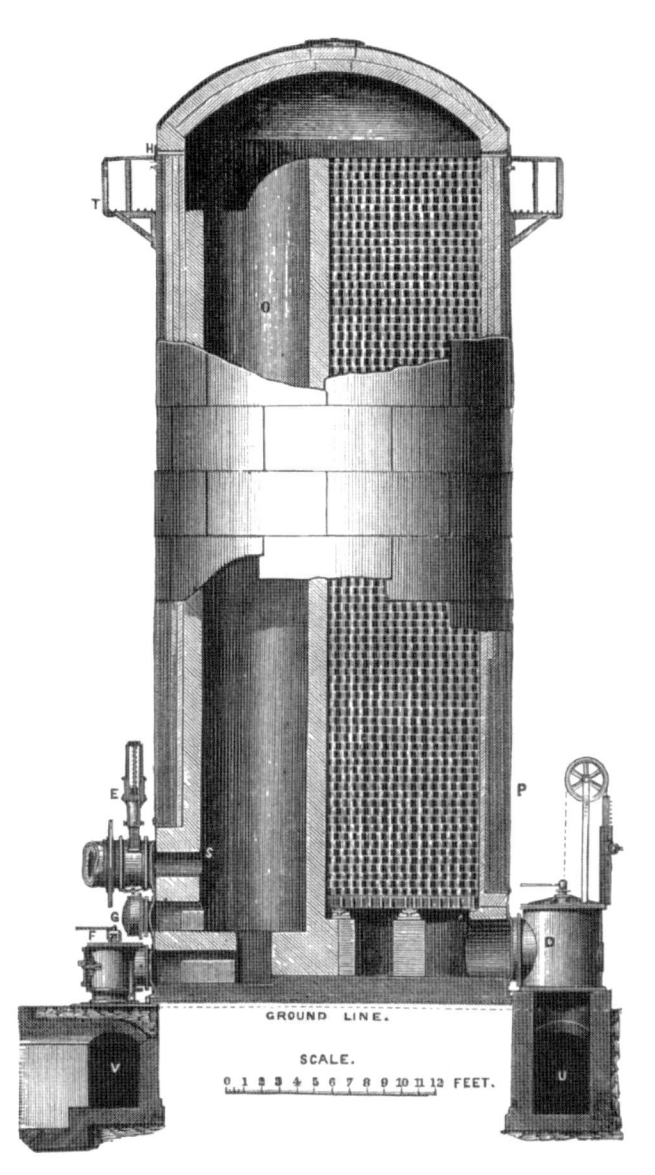

Above: *A detailed engraving of a regenerative hot-blast stove very similar to those used at both the Moss Bay and Derwent Ironworks. Rows of these tall cylindrical structures can be seen beside the taller blast furnaces at each site. The waste gases from the top of the furnaces were collected and burnt in these stoves. The heat produced is first absorbed by the honeycomb of special bricks in each stove, in much the same way as a modern domestic storage heater. The blast of air required to smelt the iron in the blast furnace is then allowed to pass up through the network of hot brickwork and absorbs the stored heat.*

Overleaf: *A 1936 aerial photograph of the Moss Bay blast furnaces, viewed approximately from the south west. The blast furnaces are partially obscured by the line of eleven tall regenerative stoves, but the long gallery or platform linking the top of each furnace can be seen behind the tall chimney. In 1934, United Steel Companies decided to concentrate pig iron production at the Derwent ironworks (formerly Charles Cammell & Co.). Thereafter these Moss Bay furnaces were retained only as a standby, being used largely to produce spiegel and ferro-manganese. (Michael Burridge Collection)*

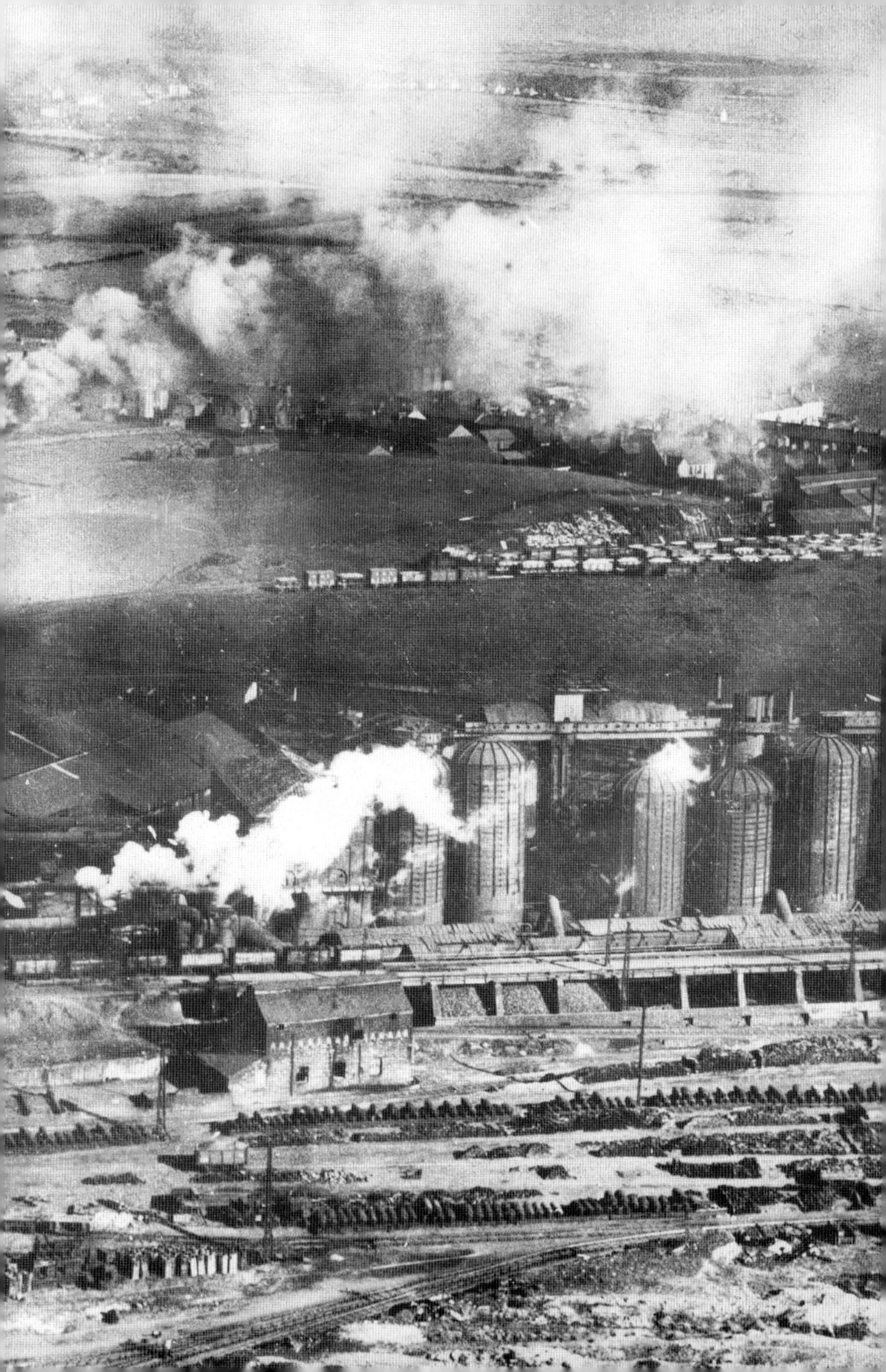

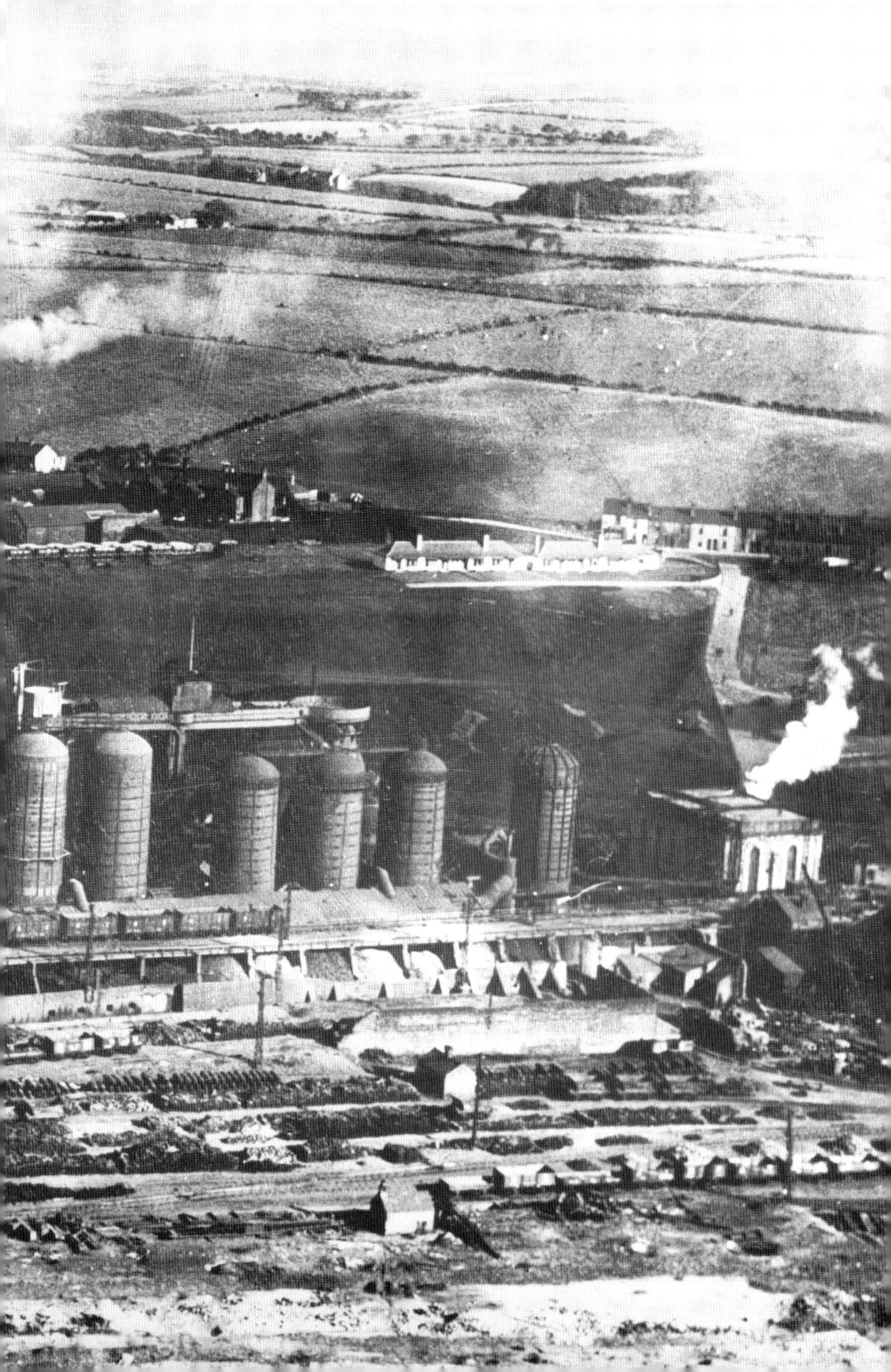

Above: *A United Steel Companies 50-ton capacity ladle used to transport the molten pig iron from the blast furnaces to the Bessemer converters at Workington works. It was supported on a special rail bogie, known as a ladle car.* (Bessemer Steel Archive)

Opposite: *The 400-ton capacity Wellman hot metal mixer, installed at Moss Bay in 1935, was located adjacent to the two new 25-ton Bessemer converters. Essentially, it held the pig iron in hot storage until it was made into steel in the converters. The mixer would also even out any slight variations in iron composition, ensuring a thoroughly uniform metal was always used. This photograph shows a 50-ton capacity ladle of molten pig iron being lifted by the overhead crane, using the wing-like horns on either side of the ladle. A chain attached close to the bottom of the raised ladle is then used to tilt and pour the iron into the mixer.* (Bessemer Steel Archive)

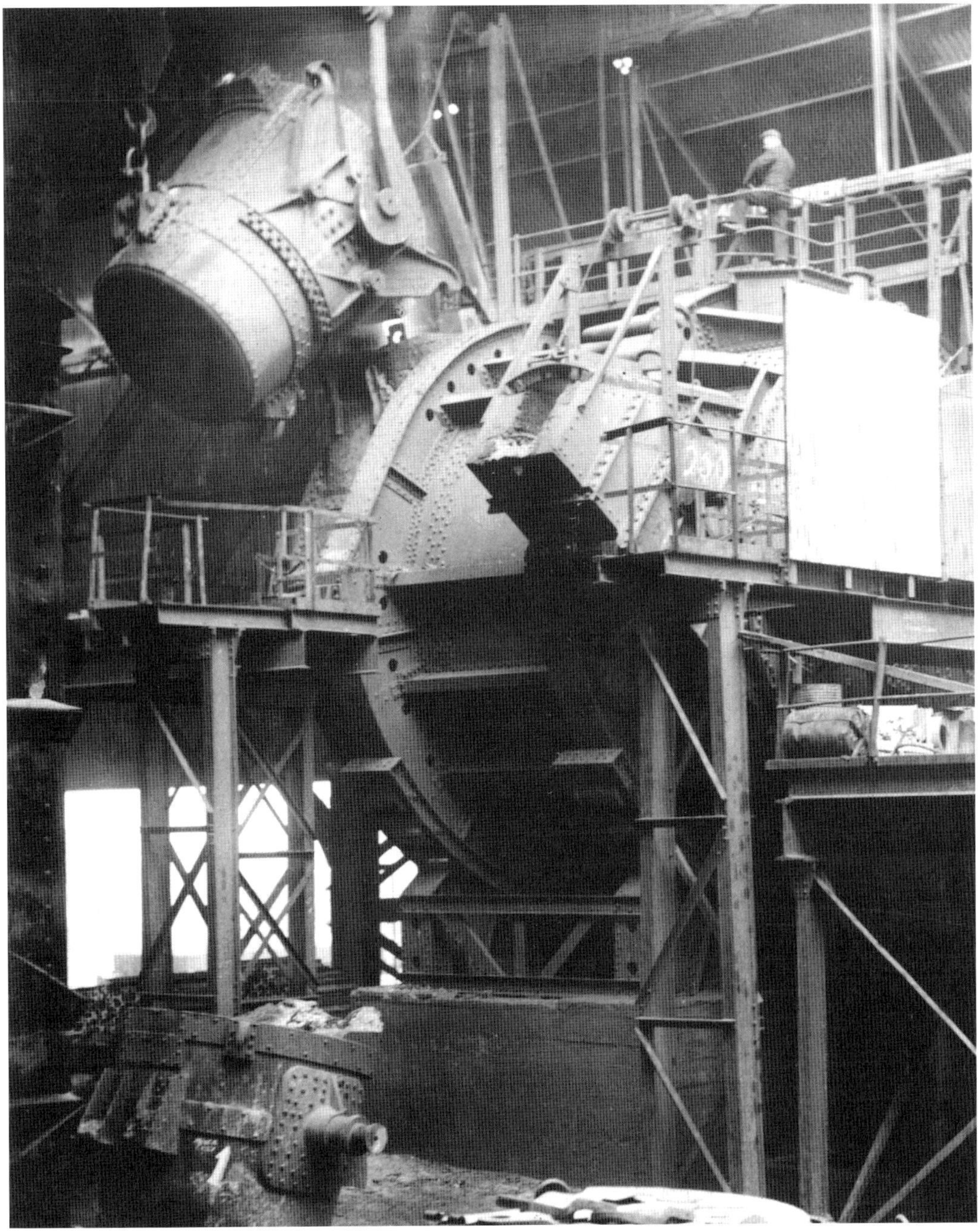

Above: A ladle of molten pig iron has been drawn from the 400-ton mixer and is charged or poured into the mouth of a 25-ton capacity Bessemer converter. Before being filled, the converter vessel is first rotated to lie almost horizontal. In this position the charge of molten iron comes to rest well away from the tuyères or air holes at the base of the converter. (Bessemer Steel Archive)

Opposite: With the converter still in its horizontal position, a powerful blast of air is introduced through the tuyères and this sweeps across the molten metal. As the pressure of the blow increases, the converter is tilted into its upright position. A furious clash of air and metal occurs, sending a shower of sparks and flames skyward. Initially, the silicon and manganese impurities in the iron are burnt away. Then the temperature rises dramatically, the flame from the mouth of the converter lengthens and becomes much brighter. As the flame reaches a length of over 30ft (10m) and attains a dazzling brilliance, the carbon deposits in the iron are burnt away. (Bessemer Steel Archive)

pp.90-1: *The two 25-ton capacity Stewart Demag Bessemer converters installed at Moss Bay in 1934. The flame of the left vessel has shortened and is turning white. This signals that all the carbon has been removed and the blow is almost completed.* (Bessemer Steel Archive)

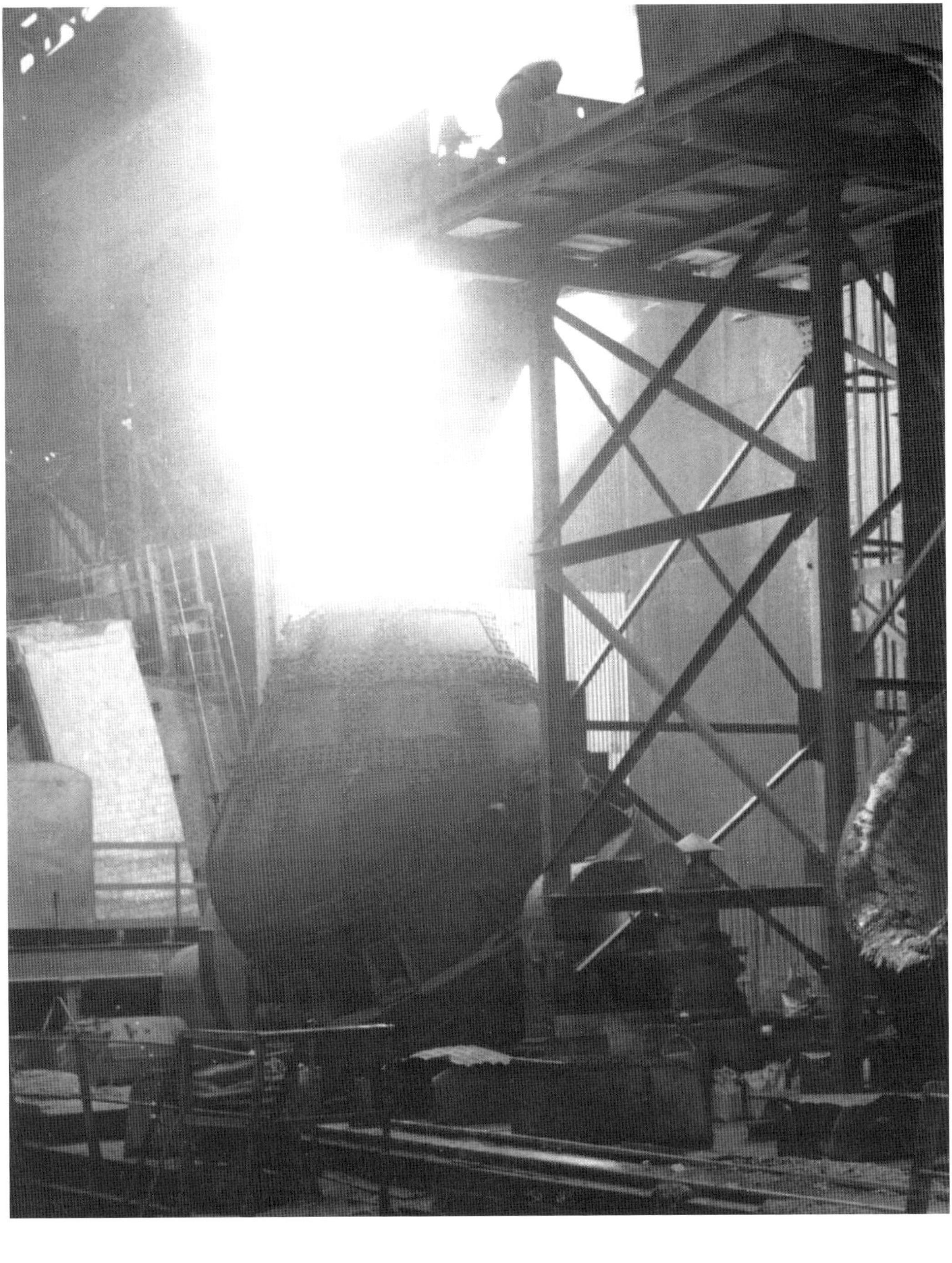

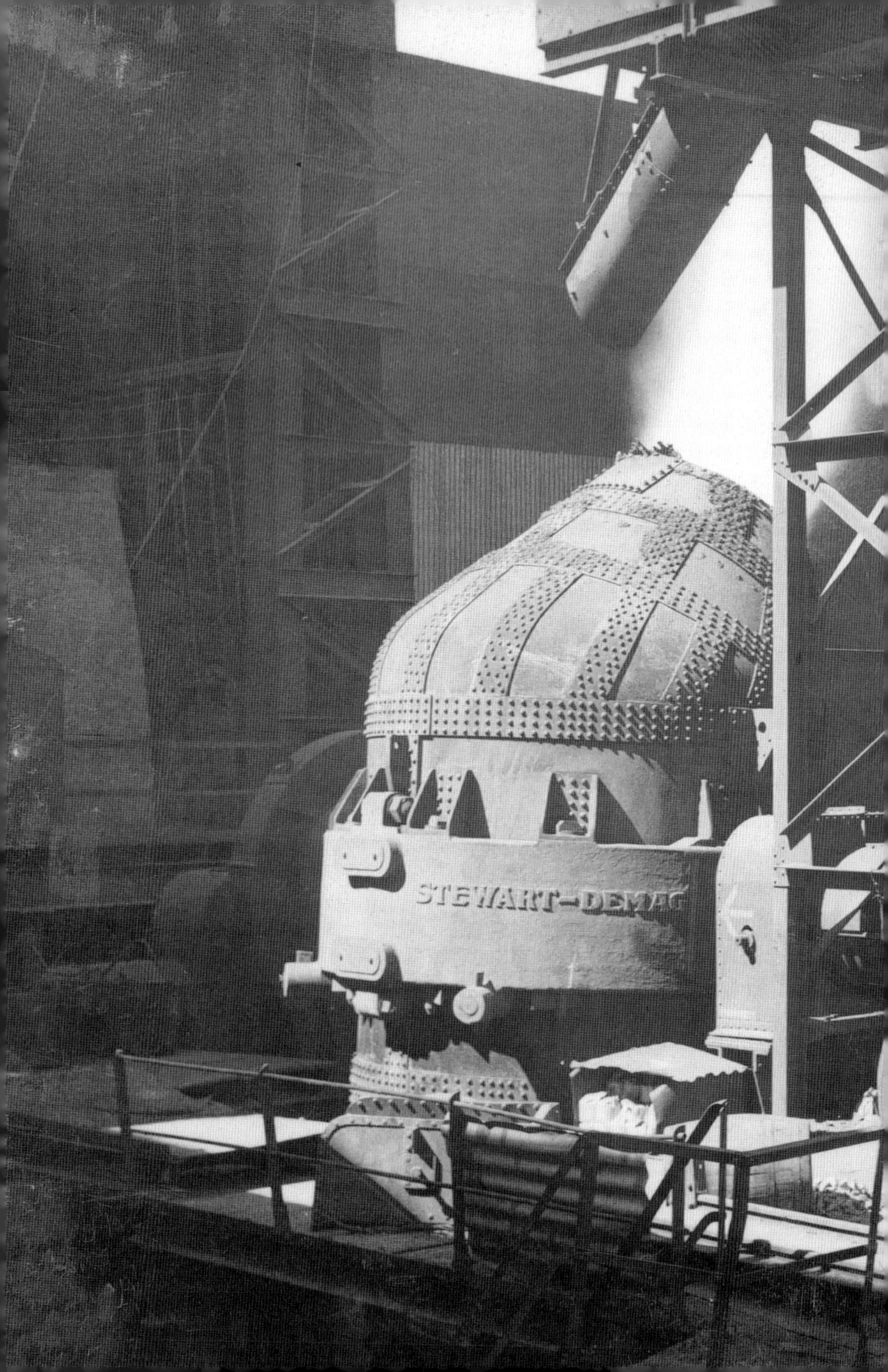
STEWART–DEMAG

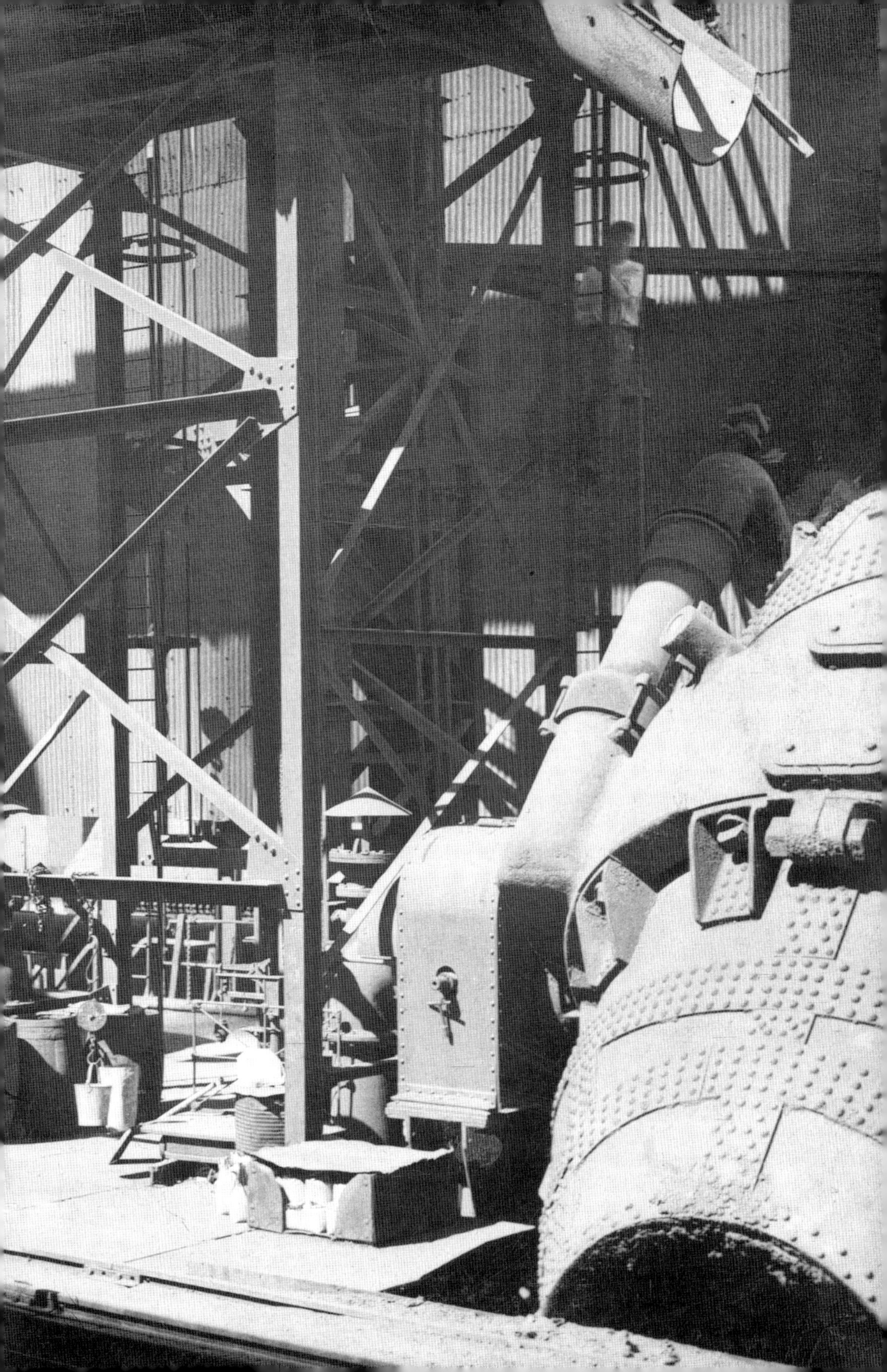

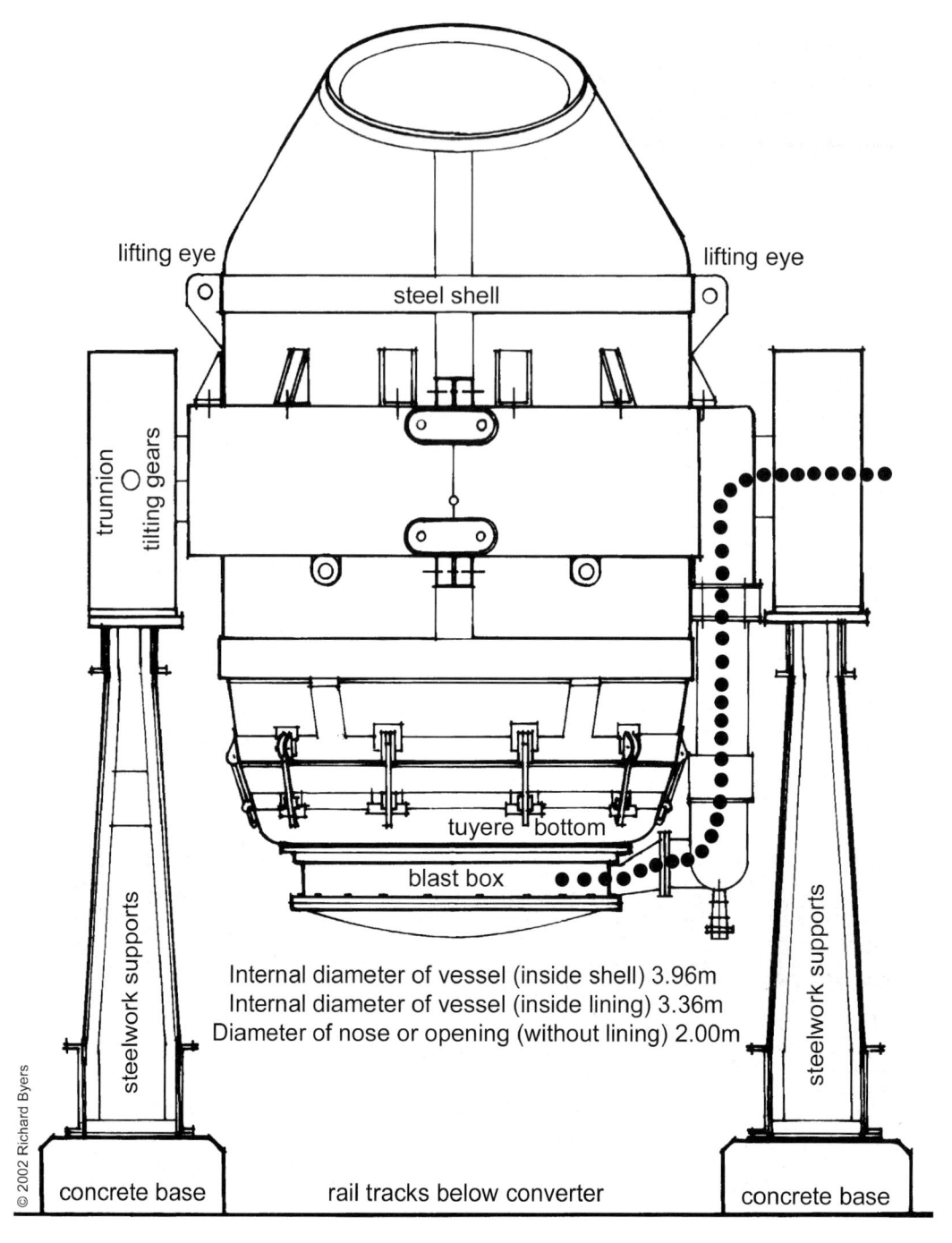

A scale drawing of one of the 25-ton capacity Stewart Demag Bessemer converters installed at Workington. The dotted line indicates how the blast of air is introduced to the tuyère bottom at the base of the vessel. The air blast pipe can also be clearly seen on the inverted vessel on the previous page. Each converter also has two lifting eyes on either side, to enable the vessel to be lifted from its supports when any repair and maintenance work is required.

After the blow is completed, the converter is rotated once more into its horizontal position. A controlled quantity of molten spiegel or spielgeleisen (a triple compound of iron, manganese and carbon) is then poured from a small ladle carried by the overhead crane. The vessel then briefly returns once again to the vertical and is rocked back and forth to ensure the steel and spiegel are thoroughly mixed. By adding spiegel, excess oxygen is removed from the molten metal and the desired grade of steel is obtained. (Bessemer Steel Archive)

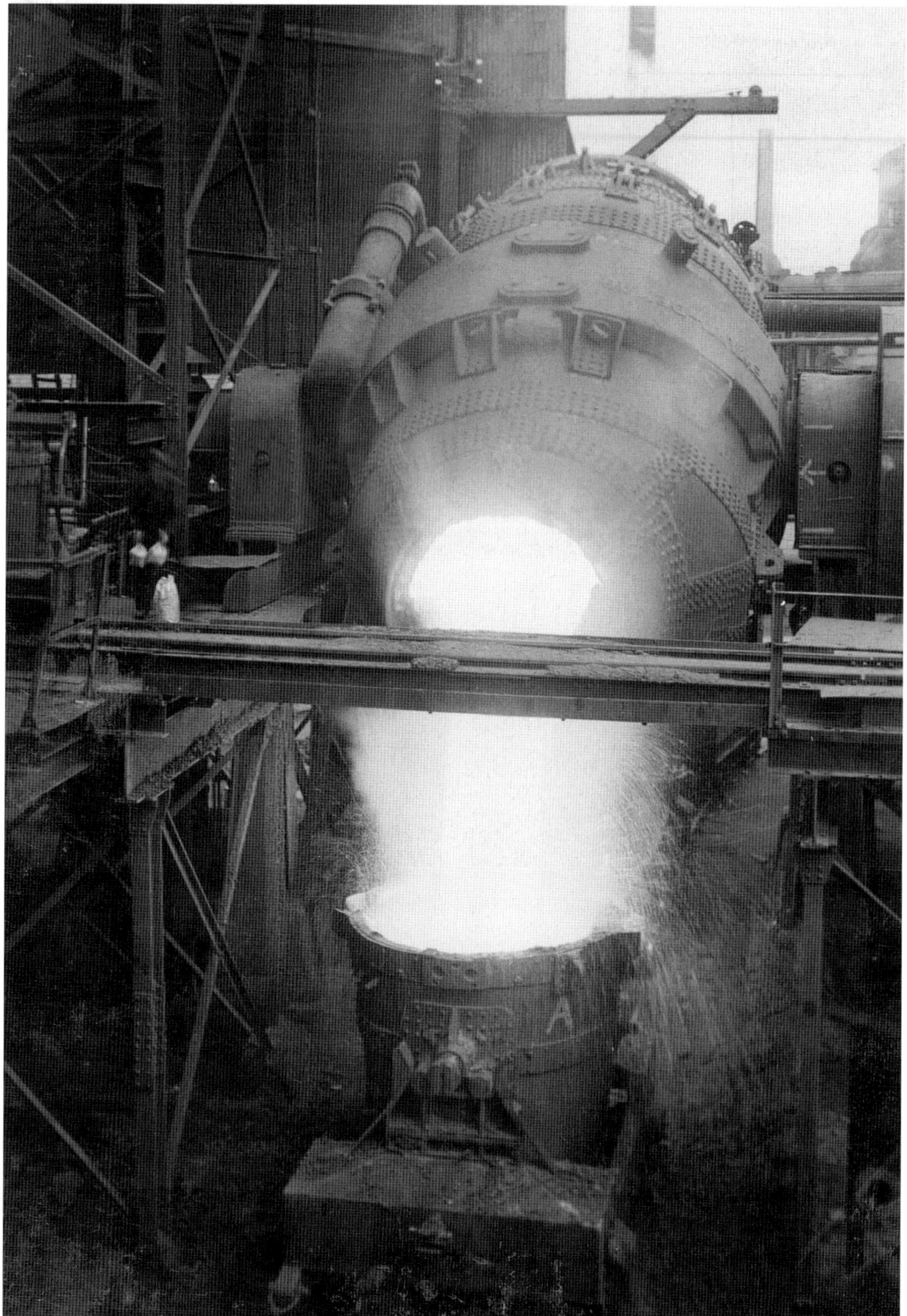

Above: *An interesting view from beneath one of the 25-ton capacity converters, as the molten steel is emptied into the teeming ladle. The valve rod on the teeming ladle can clearly be seen protruding from the right-hand side of the ladle.* (Michael Burridge Collection)

Opposite: *The molten steel is now poured off into the teeming ladle. This ladle is supported on the track-mounted transfer car beneath the vessel. It was hauled the short distance into the casting shop by a steel rope and windlass, operated by the boxman, the blower's assistant.* (Bessemer Steel Archive)

Sunlight streams through the high level windows, along the west side of the cathedral-like casting shop at Moss Bay. In 1934, as the two new 25-ton capacity converters were installed, the new casting shop was also constructed. This long building was located immediately to the south of the new Bessemer shop. In the foreground is the Wellman 4-ton stripping crane, which ran back and forth along the length of the casting shop on overhead rails. It was used to lift or strip the moulds from the ingots of steel (see p.100). (Bessemer Steel Archive)

A view of the interior of the casting shop at Moss Bay, from its south-east corner. In the foreground is an array of teeming ladles. Each was first lined internally with square 2in (50mm) thick firebrick tiles and then protected with a layer of ganister, a plaster-like silicious material applied with a trowel. This ganister lining of the ladle lasted around twelve casts, while the firebrick tiles it protected needed replacing after about 100 blows. To the left of the photograph, the teemer standing on the casting platform directs the molten steel into a row of empty ingot moulds. (Bessemer Steel Archive)

The teemer Bob Elliott standing confidently on the narrow edge of a mould, c.1936. He is controlling the flow of liquid steel into the ingot, using the valve lever on the side of the teeming ladle. The sheer size of the teeming ladle can be judged by comparison with the man beside it. (Bessemer Steel Archive)

A view of the interior of the casting shop at the Moss Bay Bessemer steel plant on 26 July 1974, the last day of steel production at Workington. A large crowd, made up of many retired employees and the present workforce, gathered to witness this historic and rather sad event. (British Steel Corporation)

All eyes gaze skyward towards the converter as the last blow brightly illuminates the casting shop for the very last time. The emotional crowd fell silent as the flame receded, tough and proud steelworkers struggling the holding back a tear in their eyes. After over a century, steelmaking at Workington had ended forever.

The Bessemer steel plant at Moss Bay was then dismantled, and so too were the redundant Derwent blast furnaces which had smelted many thousands of tons of pig iron. In November 1980 the last of the old converter vessels, now rusting and redundant, left the town and was moved to Sheffield. It was erected at the entrance to the newly opened Kelham Island Industrial Museum and can still be seen there today. (British Steel Corporation)

Empty ingot moulds assembled on their rail cars within the Bessemer casting shop. The ingot moulds varied in size and design depending on the desired grade or type of steel. At Workington, the steel was generally cast into tall square open-bottom moulds. The internal faces of the moulds were also designed to taper upwards to aid removal. On the upper outside edge were projecting lugs which were used by the stripper crane to lift the mould away from the solidified steel ingot. (Michael Burridge Collection)

A white-hot ingot of steel is lifted from the soaking pits at Moss Bay, c.1936. The newly cast ingots of steel were brought from the casting shop to the soaking pits by rail. Within the soaking pits, the ingots were literally soaked with heat, to even out any temperature variations prior to rolling. The rolling process was only successful if the steel was at a uniform temperature throughout. (Bessemer Steel Archive)

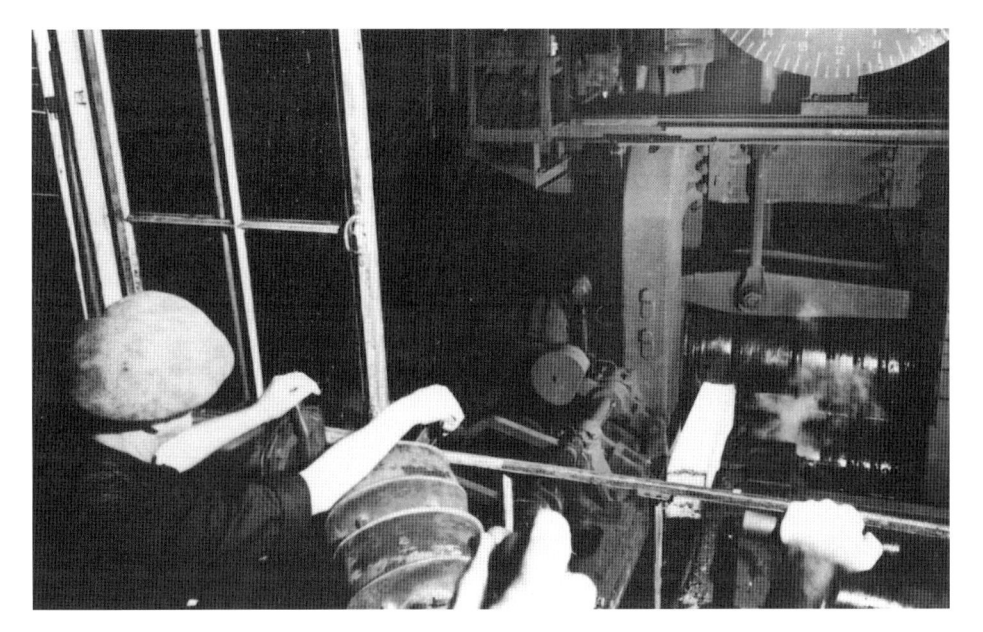

The white-hot ingot or bloom of steel is now passed through the rollers of the cogging or breakdown mill (or stand). This is the first stage of the rolling process, where the cross-section of the bloom is reduced to a more suitable size for rolling. The back-and-forth motion of the bloom through the rollers is controlled from a high level pulpit or box overlooking the rolling mill. (Bessemer Steel Archive)

A white-hot ingot or bloom of steel is passed back and forth through a series of specially designed heavy rollers in the rolling mill, a device that has been likened to a huge mangle, similar to that once used by every household on washing day. This process basically squeezes and shapes the ingot into a long rail. (Michael Burridge Collection)

A closer look at the rollers of the finishing mill or stand. This series of heavy rollers forms the rail into its final cross-section. Before this stage, the bloom has already made several passes through the rollers of cogging and roughing mills. First the cogging or breakdown mill, as it is sometimes called, reduces the bloom to a suitable cross-section for the rail or section being produced. It is then transferred to the roughing mill and gradually rolled into the approximate shape of the finished rail. The bloom typically makes fifteen passes through these three rolling mills before emerging as a finished rail. (Michael Burridge Collection)

Finished steel railway lines stacked in rail banks at Moss Bay, ready for despatch to the customer. Since November 1872, Workington has supplied many thousands of miles of railway lines to almost every rail network in the world. (Michael Burridge Collection)

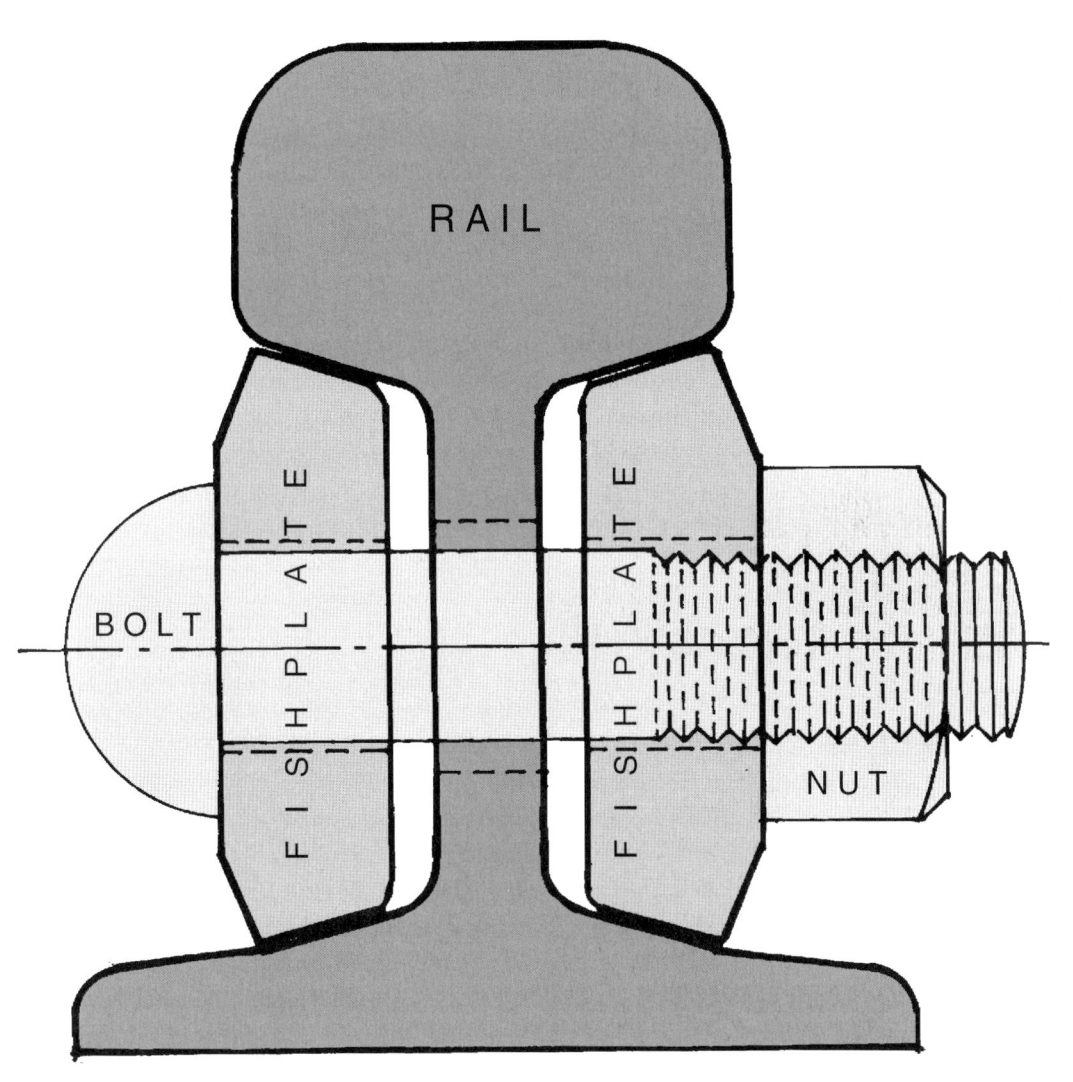

A cross-section through a standard flat-bottom steel rail made at Workington. This is typical of the railway lines made at Moss Bay for over a century. When the track is laid, each rail length is joined to the next by fishplates. These short lengths of almost flat steel section (usually around 23½in [600mm] long) are placed on both sides of the rail, spanning the join and bolted together through the flange. By the 1950s, Workington was the largest British producer of permanent way products, supplying nearly a third of the track used by British Rail.

After the molten steel has been poured off into the teeming ladle (see pages 94-95), the converter vessel is fully inverted and rocked to remove the slag or waste residue. This is transported away in shallow slag pans along the rails beneath the converter, drawn by a small electric locomotive. This slag was usually dumped along the Moss Bay shoreline, along with other waste from the blast furnaces. The empty converter would now be inspected and any necessary repairs carried out before the next blow. (Bessemer Steel Archive)

A 1960s aerial photograph of the Workington coastline to the south of the River Derwent estuary. The Workington Iron & Steel Co. Moss Bay steelworks can be seen in the distance, whilst the Distington Engineering Co. works are to the left of the photograph. In the centre, looking almost moonlike, are the massive slag banks and spoil heaps towering above the coastline. A man-made legacy of almost a century of iron- and steel-making in the town.

Above: *Tuyères for the removable bottom plug of the 25-ton capacity Bessemer converters being made at United Steel Companies' Micklam brickworks, c.1950. These were shaped from extruded lengths of fireclay in tall cylindrical moulds. The air holes in the tuyère were formed by driving a series of rods through the length of the wet clay, prior to firing in the kiln.* (Helena Thompson Museum)

Opposite: *Ruben Weir and Spud Murphy repair the tuyère bottom (or Holley bottom) of one of the 25-ton capacity Bessemer converters, c.1955. The vessel is almost horizontal and the blast box bottom has been removed. The tuyère plug of these larger converters was of 8ft 7in (2620mm) diameter and contained up to thirty individual firebrick tuyères. The earlier 16-ton capacity converters (see pages 46-51) had a much smaller plug. It was just 4ft 7in (1410mm) diameter with nineteen or twenty-four tuyères. These bottom plugs were made on site at Workington. The individual tuyères were arranged in a circular mould and the space between them filled with crushed firebrick and fireclay. The entire plug was then firmly pressed with a pneumatic rammer. It was then removed from its mould and fired in a kiln or oven for several days.* (Bessemer Steel Archive)

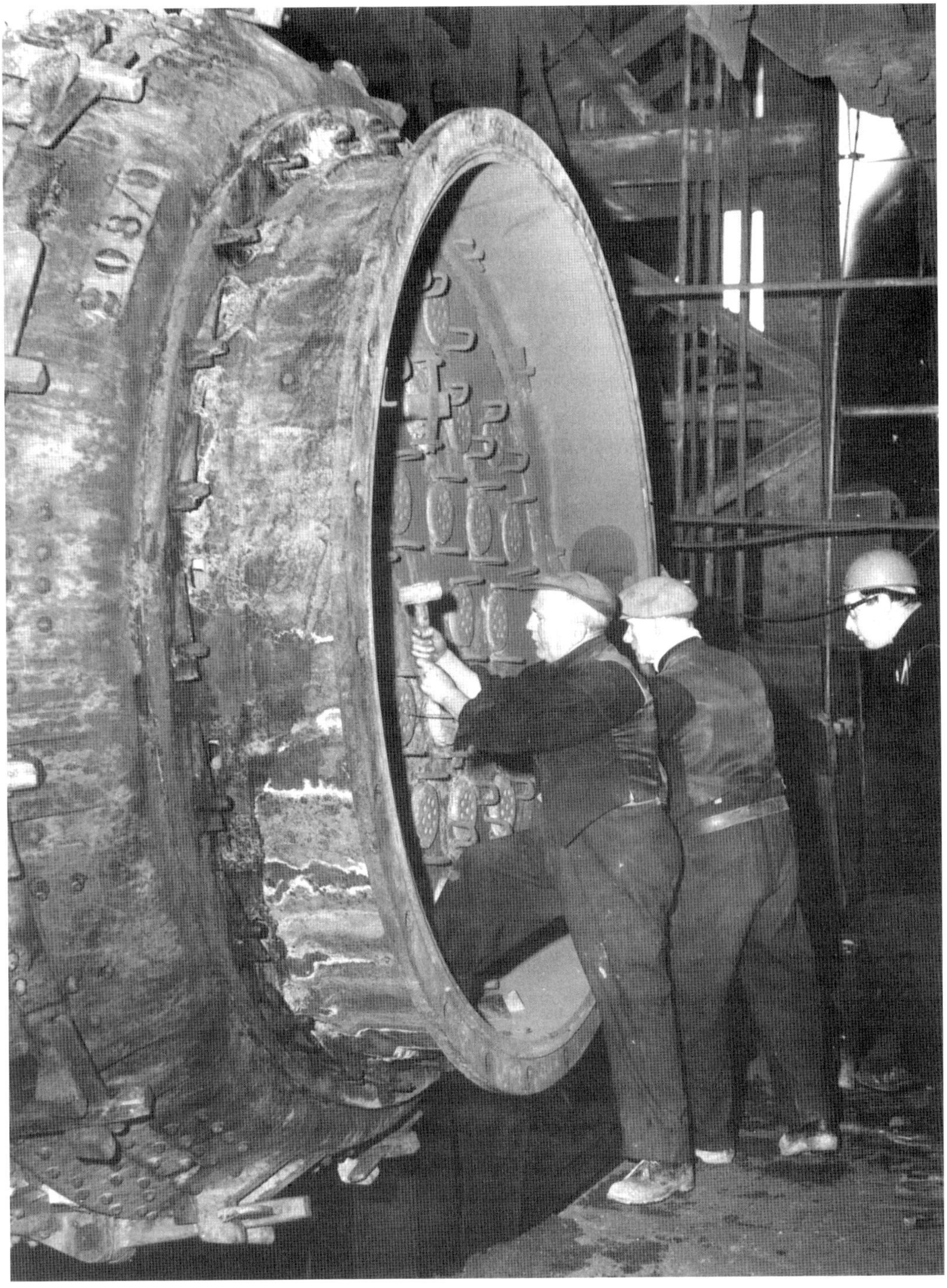

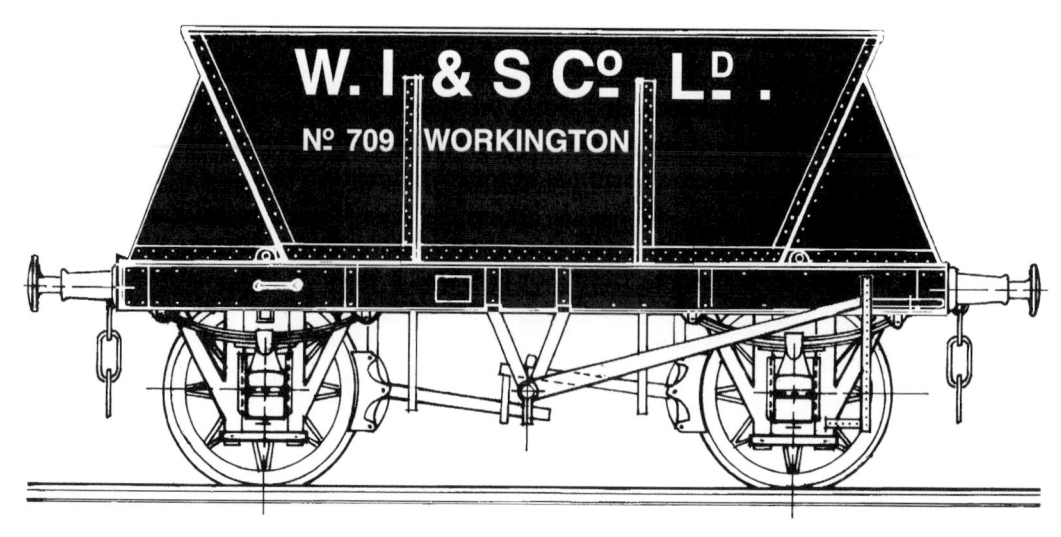

Scale drawing of a 15-ton steel hopper wagon, built for the Workington Iron & Steel Co., by Charles Roberts of Wakefield. These privately owned wagons had a distinctive black livery with white signage and wheel rims. They would generally have carried iron ore, coal or coke to the works from the local collieries and mines. The ends and sides of the hopper body were constructed from slanting sheeting. Each wagon was fitted with brakes on both sides, and had grease axleboxes and spoked wheels.

Workington Iron & Steel Co. locomotive No.69, an 0–4–0 saddle tank steam engine built at the Robert Stephenson Locomotive Works. (Helena Thompson Museum)

In 1936, a new coke oven plant was built to the north of the Derwent blast furnaces for the United Steel Companies by the Woodall Ducklam Co. Initially it consisted of fifty-three individual ovens, by the 1950s there were sixty-four. These ovens to the left of the photograph were capable of producing all the blast furnace coke required for smelting iron at Workington. A by-product of this coke production was gas, which was initially sold in bulk to the borough council. They were then responsible for supplying gas to virtually all the town's domestic and trade consumers. After the gas industry was nationalised in May 1949, United Steel continued to supply the newly formed National Gas Board. Much of the coal used at the coke ovens was mined at the nearby Solway Colliery. (Michael Burridge Collection)

Above: *Not all the pig iron produced by the blast furnaces was sent to the Bessemer converters for steelmaking. Blast furnaces ran almost continuously by design, whilst there were often fluctuations in the demand for steel. Originally, the excess smelted iron would have been simply drawn from the blast furnace and cast into pigs (or blocks) in sand-lined pig beds. In 1935–36, United Steel Companies built a new pig-casting machine at Workington, which superseded this older casting method. This photograph shows a 50-ton capacity ladle of molten pig iron being poured into this new pig-casting building.*

Opposite above: *The molten pig iron from the tilted ladle, on the left, then flows down a short channel to the foot of the double strand of moulds or pans.*

Opposite below: *The pig-iron moulds were attached to each other in a long chain. As each pan was filled, another row was moved into place beneath the stream of molten metal.*

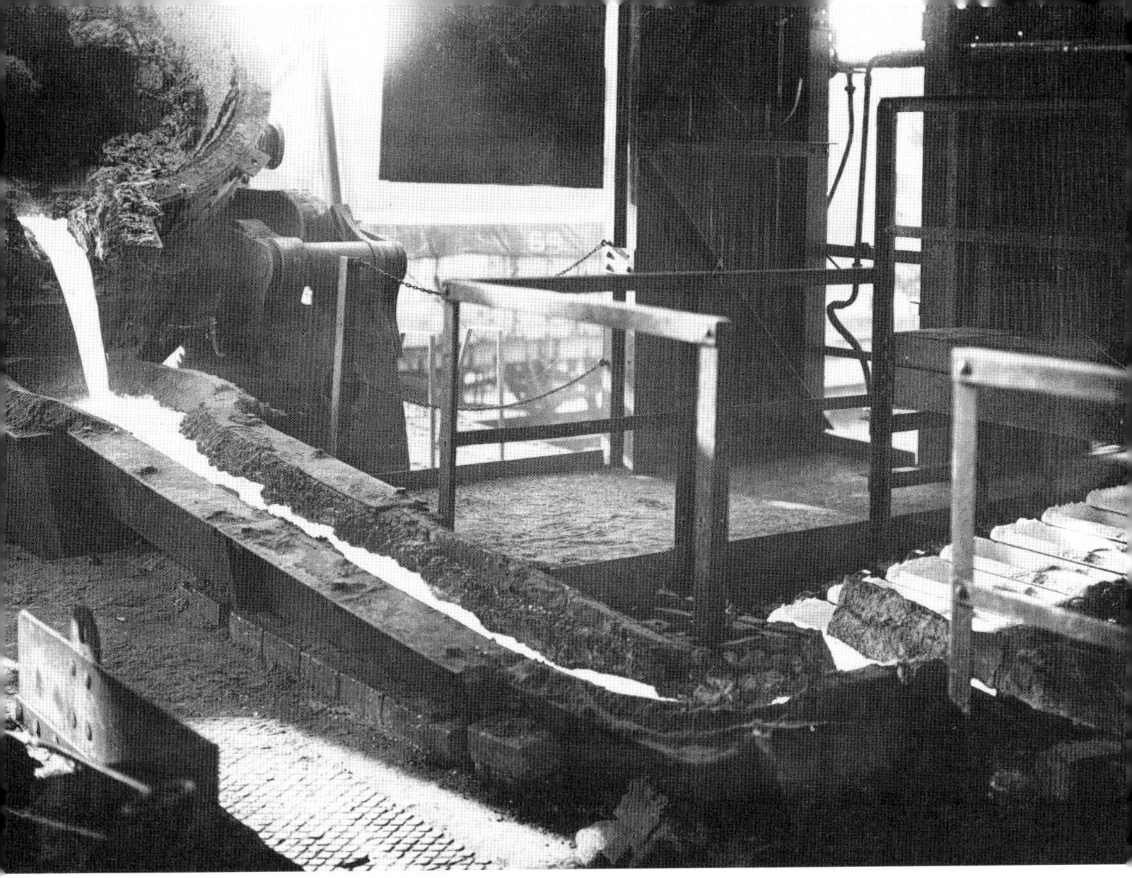

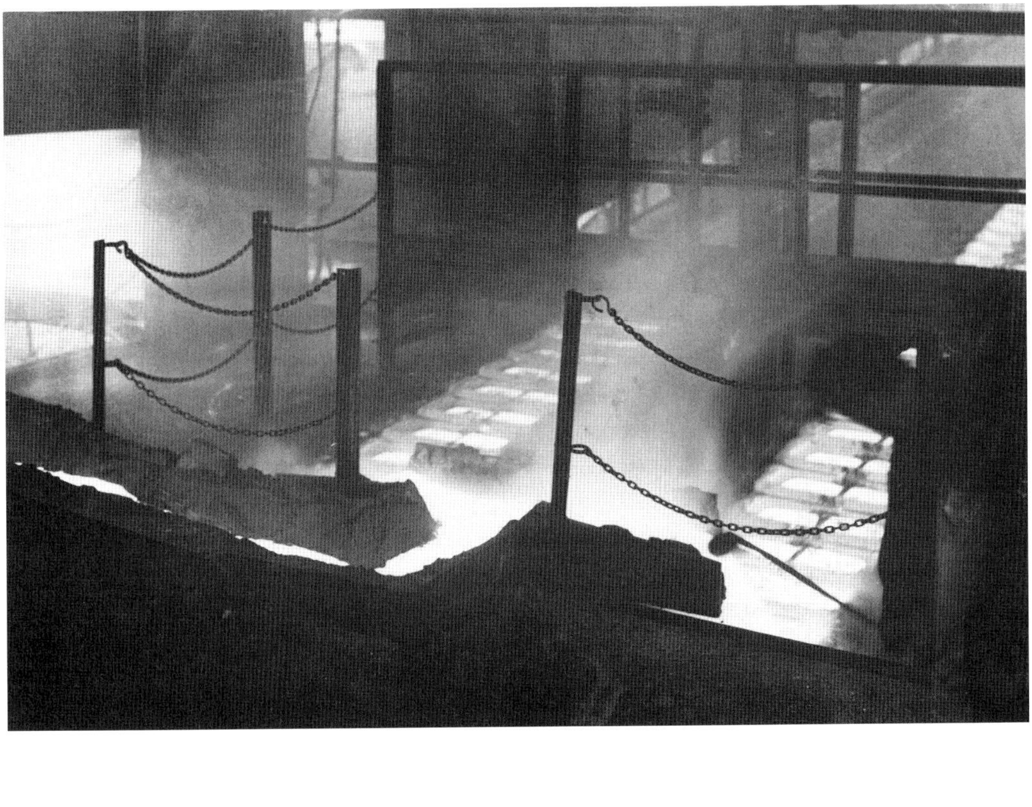

An exterior view of the pig-casting machine, c.1940. The process of filling the rows of individual moulds seen on the preceding pages was carried out to the right of this picture. The line of pans extended up through the inclined section of this building. By the time they reached the top the pig iron had solidified in its mould.

Within the taller structure, the pans were inverted and the moulded blocks of pig iron were simply allowed to fall into a railway wagon below. They were obviously still very hot, and water sprays were used to cool the castings.

Another view along the exterior of the pig-casting machine building, c.1940, this time viewed from the opposite direction. In the foreground to the left, amidst the clouds of steam, water sprays cool the newly cast ingots as they fall into the railway wagons below. In the distance at the other end of the structure is the tilted ladle of pig iron shown in more detail on p.110.

A close-up photograph of the moulds of the pig-casting machine. These pans were connected in a long continuous band or chain which ran the entire length of the incline section of the building. When each mould was emptied at the top of the machine, it would move back down the underside of the slope to be refilled once more.

A 1999 aerial photograph of Corus Rail's Moss Bay site. The existing rail bank can be seen in the centre of the photograph. The old Derwent Ironworks, acquired by Charles Cammell & Co. in 1882, was immediately to the north of the Moss Bay works. The large reservoir is perhaps the only remaining feature of this once

prominent plant. The Derwent blast furnaces were built on the north-west side of this pond and are shown in more detail on pp. 72-3.

An exterior view of the Workington Iron & Steel Co. rail-finishing plant at Moss Bay, c.1960, viewed from the east. Here the rails were straightened and accurately cut to length, and other finishing operations were performed, such as drilling or grinding. In the foreground is the main Harrington–Workington railway line. Between the railway tracks and the buildings of the steelworks is the rail bank still used today by Corus Rail, Workington.

Above: *A strip of steel plate passes through the heavy Loewy Press and emerges as a steel railway sleeper, formed into its final shape. The inverted sleeper is in the centre of the photograph. Throughout its long history, Workington has produced many hundreds of thousands of such sleepers to suit rail sections between 45lb/yd and 110lb/yd (22.5kg/m and 54.5kg/m).* (Michael Burridge Collection)

Right: *Steel railway sleepers have been manufactured at Moss Bay since 1884. They are used extensively throughout the world as an alternative to the conventional creosoted timber sleeper. A Moss Bay steel railway sleeper (dated 1899) is currently displayed at the town's Helena Thompson Museum.* (Michael Burridge Collection)

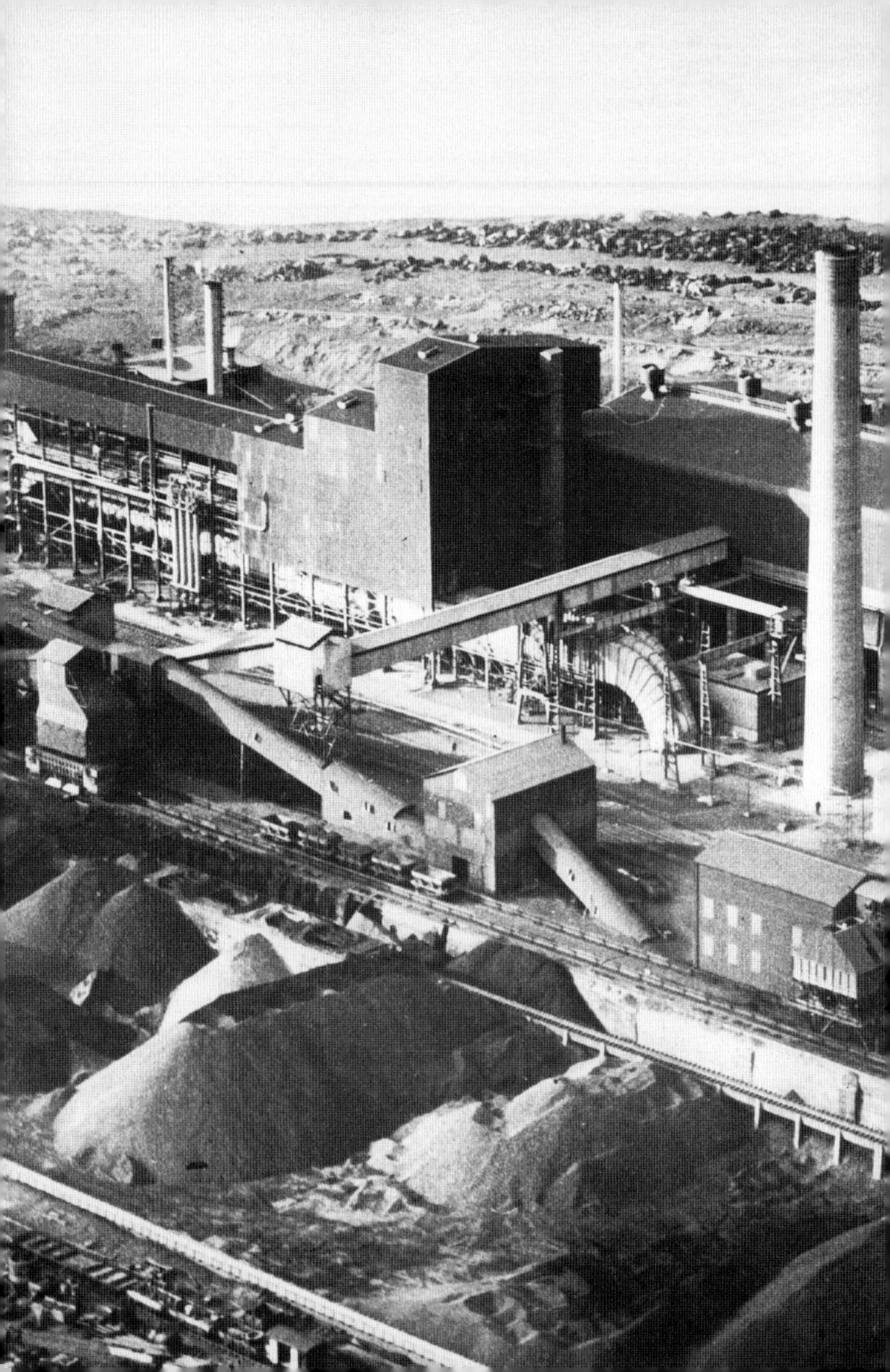

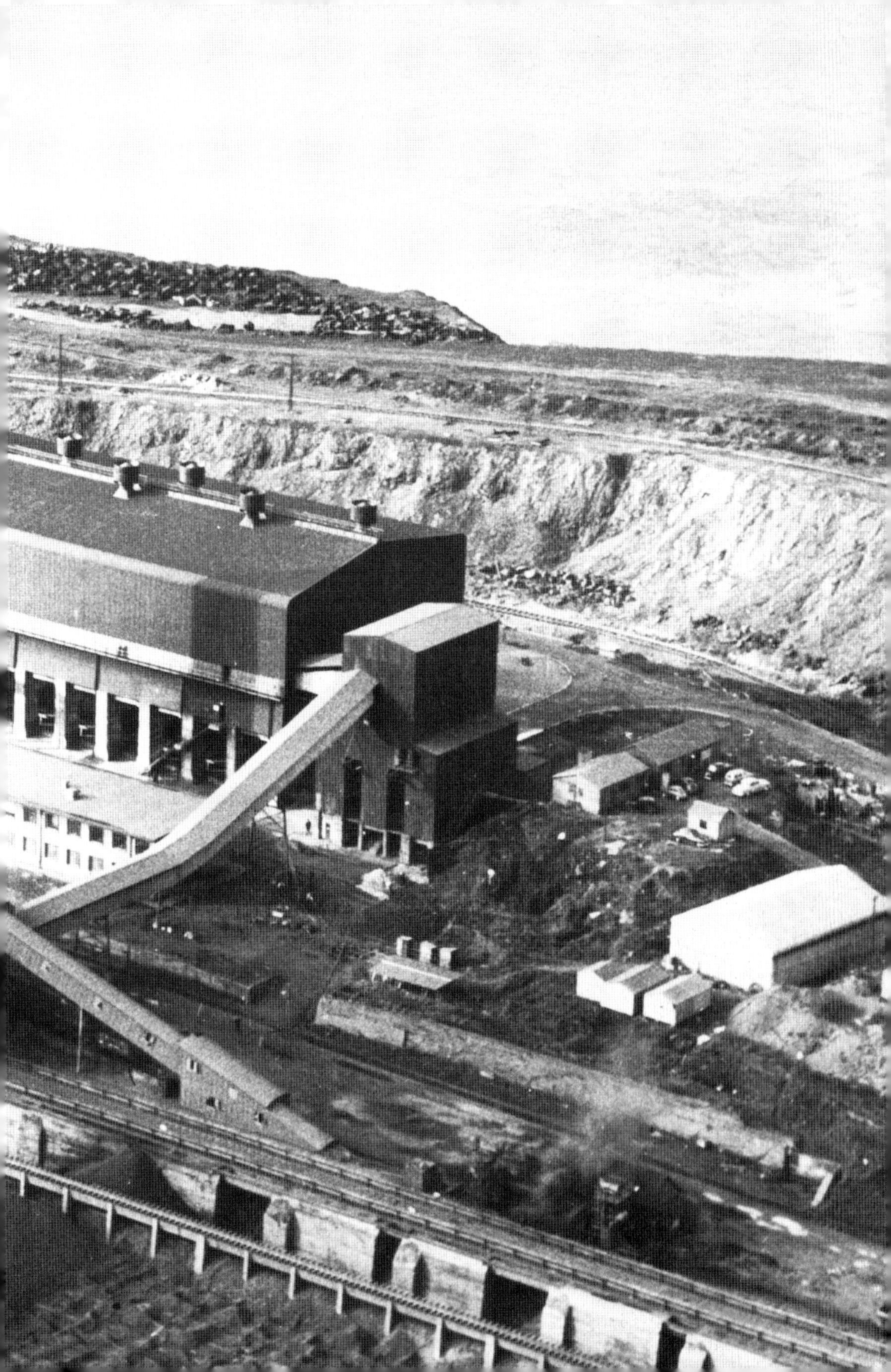

Above: *The relatively modern underground workings of the Solway Colliery sunk by United Steel Companies in 1937. Costing in the region of £486,000, the pit was an integral part of the iron and steel works, supplying much of the coal used in the coke ovens. After the coal industry was nationalised in 1947, the colliery passed to the National Coal Board. Its closure in 1973 signalled the end of coal mining in the town.* (Michael Burridge Collection)

Previous spread: *The sinter plant at Workington Iron & Steel Works, viewed from the north-east. Sintering was gradually introduced after the Second World War, and was used to prepare haematite iron ores before they were charged into the blast furnaces. When smelting in a blast furnace, the material should not pack together so tightly that the flow of the air blast and by-product gases is impeded. The sinter plant process basically now allowed smaller ores to be used and also reduced the levels of sulphur, calcium and bituminous impurities in the haematite. It produced cubes of ore of a fairly standard and usable size, with an open, fissured and porous condition, ideal for smelting.* (Eric Martin Collection)

Naphthalene house, benzole dock, tanks and house, cooling frame, boiler house and scrubbers. Before the gas from the coke ovens could be safely supplied to the town, it had to be cleaned (or scrubbed). This plant was installed to remove, recover and process the crude benzole in the gas. It was then stored in the 100,000 cu.ft gas holder to the left of the photograph, before being released into the main. (Michael Burridge Collection)

The interior of the machine shop at the Distington Engineering Co., c.1950. This modern foundry was also owned by the United Steel Companies and is more commonly known as the Chapel Bank works. By the 1960s, the plant was the largest iron foundry in Europe, employing over 300 men. (Michael Burridge Collection)

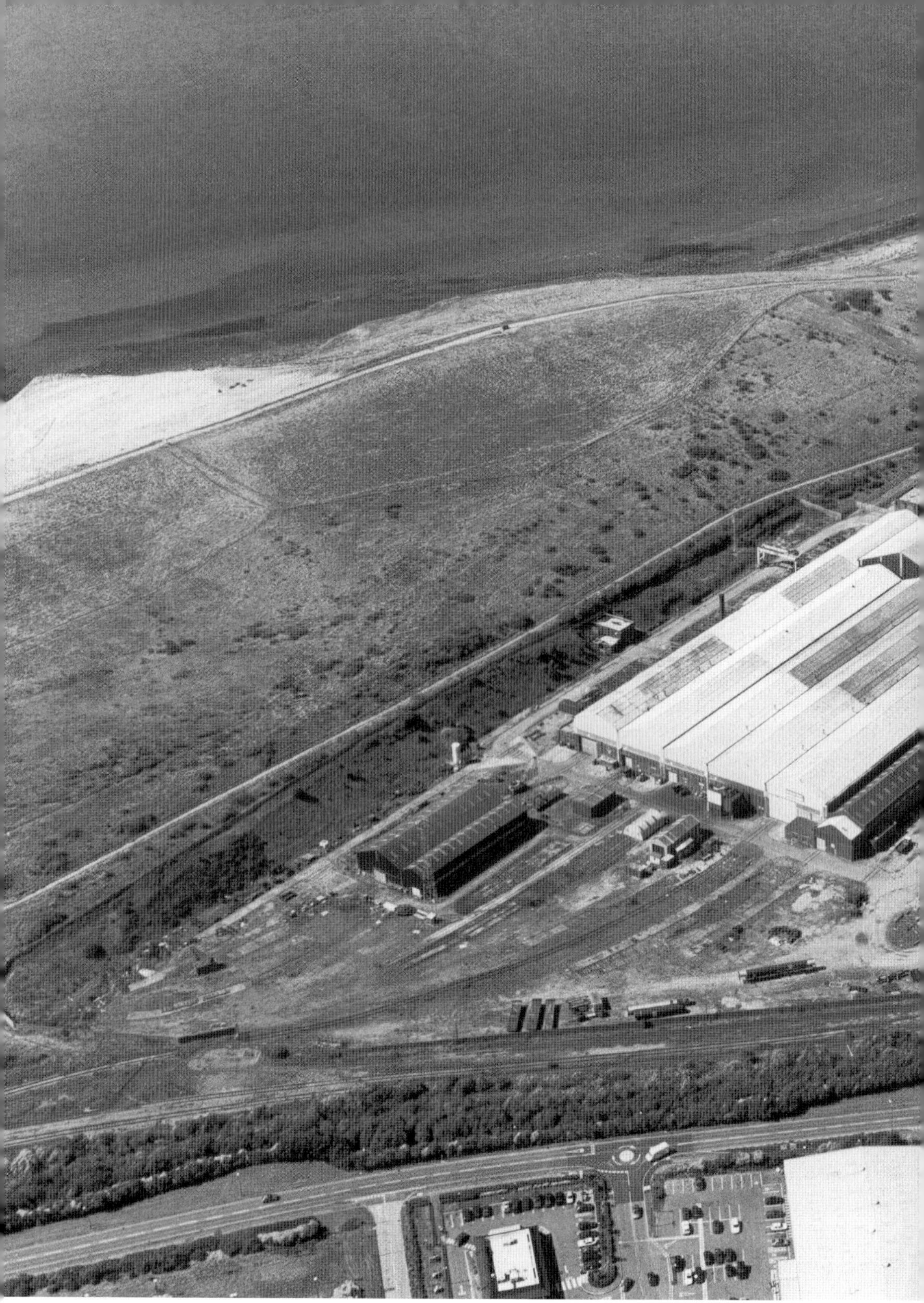

A 1999 aerial photograph showing the Distington Engineering Co. works, located just to the south of the mouth of the River Derwent. The plant is now operated by Corus Engineering.

Bibliography

Austin, John, & Ford, Malcolm, *Steel Town: Dronfield and Wilson Cammell* (Scarsdale, 1983)
Baggley, Philip, & Sanderson, Neil, *Bessemer Steel: Pictorial Archive of Steelmaking at Workington* (Richard Byers, 2002)
Bulmer, T., & Co., *History and Trade Directory of Cumberland* (1901)
Burridge, Michael, *Steelmaking in West Cumberland* (unpublished notes, 1963)
Burrow, E.J., *The Seaport Town of Workington and it's development* (E.J. Burrow, c.1916)
Byers, Richard L.M., *History of Workington from earliest times to 1865* (Richard Byers, 1998)
Byers, Richard L.M., *History of Workington, 1866–1955* (Richard Byers, 2002)
Cleator & Workington Junction Railway – original minute books 1875–1923
Cumberland Pacquet (various issues from 1866 onwards)
Daysh, G.H.J. & Watson, Evelyn M., *Cumberland: A Survey of Industrial Facilities* (Cumberland Development Council, 1951)
Gilbert, Martin, *Second World War* (George Weinfield & Nicholson, 1989)
Heal, David W., *The Steel Industry in Post War Britain* (David & Charles, 1974)
Lancaster, J.Y., & Wattleworth, D.R., *The Iron and Steel Industry of West Cumberland* (British Steel, 1977)
Lloyd George, David, *War Memoirs of David Lloyd George* (Odhams Press)
Keeling, B.S., & Wright, A.E.G., *The Development of Modern Iron and Steel Industry* (Longmans, 1964)
Maryport & Workington Advertiser (various issues from 1884)
Mining Manual and Mining Yearbook (1924)
Smith, David Burrand, *Huntrods Family History* (1998)
Suart, George, *Suart's Almamac* (George Suart, Wilson Street, Workington, 1895)
Sugden, Edward Haigh, *History of Arlecdon & Frizington* (Richard Byers, 1997)
Varty & Co., *Workington Yearbook* (1908)
Wattleworth, Douglas R., *Origin and Development of Iron and Steel Industry in West Cumberland* (paper published 1965)
West Cumberland Journal
West Cumberland Times
Whitehaven News
Workington Iron & Steel Co. Bulletins (c.1959–64)
Workington Town Council (Minutes of Council and Committees)

Index

Alloy 79
America 21, 28, 42, 45, 79
Annie Pit 56
Annie Pit Lane 56, 57, 58
Argentina 68
Arlecdon 29, 30
Armstrong, John Snowdon 70
Austin & Ford 63

Bankfield 42, 45
Banklands 42
Banklands colliery 56
Bar iron 12, 56
Barbour, Thomas 63
Barclay, Andrew 35
Barepot 7, 8, 10, 11, 12, 15, 16
Barepot Ironworks *see* Seaton Ironworks
Barepotts meadow 11
Belgian Railways 68
Benzole 109
Bessemer Gold Medal 29
Bessemer casting shop 96, 98, 100
Bessemer converter(s) 26, 28, 29, 41, 46, 47, 48, 49, 50, 51, 60, 62, 63, 68, 71, 77, 81, 86, 88, 92, 93, 94, 95, 104, 106, 107
Bessemer process 21, 23, 50, 60, 86-90
Bessemer shop 47, 48, 52, 70, 78
Bessemer, Henry 7, 21, 22, 28, 54
Bibliography 124
Bigrigg 68
Blast furnace(s) 7, 10, 11, 12, 15, 18, 19, 20, 23, 24, 26, 27, 29, 30, 31, 32, 35, 36, 40, 41, 43, 44, 58, 59, 62, 65, 66, 67, 68, 70, 71, 74, 77, 78, 79, 80, 81, 82, 83, 84, 86, 110, 120
Blast furnace Men's Union 75
Blooms 52
Boiler plate 32
Bombay 43
Bonnafoux 60
Borough of Workington 59, 70, 109
Borough surveyor 75
Boxman 95
Boykin, John 45

Bradbury, Samuel 68
Breakdown mill 52, 101, 102
Briggs, Samuel Sandys 15
Brigham 31
British Rail 103
British Steel Corporation 69, 83, 98, 99
Brussels 68
Buddle pit 65
Burnyeat, William 47, 71

Cammell Laird & Co. 61, 62, 68, 71
Cammell family 67
Cannons 12, 13
Cape, Thomas 75
Cast iron 13, 79
Casting pit 49, 62
Casting shop 77, 96, 98
Central Station 43
Chapel Bank works 79, 81, 121
Chapel Town 57
Charles Cammell & Co. 7, 57, 58, 60, 61, 62, 64, 65, 67, 68, 83, 116
Churchill, Winston 79
Clay Flatts 56
Cleator & Workington Junction Railway (C&WJR) 36, 43, 76
Clifton 11, 31
Clifton Colliery 31
Cloffolks 37
Coal 7, 30, 108, 120
Coat of arms 70
Cockermouth & Workington Railway (C&WR) 10, 15
Cockermouth, Keswick & Penrith Railway (CK&PR) 46, 76
Cogging mill 52, 81, 83, 101, 102
Coke 11, 12, 28
Coke oven gas 109
Coke ovens 59, 70, 77, 109, 120
Collieries 13, 108
Cockermouth 76
Corus Engineering 79, 123
Corus Rail 7, 8, 40, 43, 116
Cumberland 63
Cumberland Coal Miners' Assoc. 75
Cumberland County Council 76

Cumberland Iron Ore Miners' Assoc. 75
Cumberland Union Bank 47
Cumberland coalfield 7
Curwen family 57
Curwen, Henry Fraser 32, 41
Curwen, John Christian 13
Cyclops and Penistone works 67

Danks puddling process 29
Dearham, Robert 11
Deighton, William 41
Derbyshire 67, 68
Derwent Haematite Iron Co. 15, 63
Derwent House 10, 12
Derwent Ironworks 15, 44, 61, 62, 65, 66, 67, 68, 70, 71, 77, 80, 81, 83, 116
Derwent Park 38
Derwent Street 65
Derwent Tinplate works 15
Derwent blast furnaces 78, 79, 80, 81, 109, 116
Distington 81
Distington Engineering Co. 81, 105, 121, 123
Distington Haematite Iron Co. 79, 81
Distington Hall 81
Dixon & Bayliss 59
Dowlais Iron & Steel works 26, 29
Dronfield 63, 67, 68
Dronnies 68
Duckbill loaders 81
Duffield, James 67, 68
Duffy, T. Gavin 75
Dunkirk 79
Durham Miners Strike 36, 47

Electric-arc furnace(s) 79
Ellen Rolling Mills 59
Elliott, Bob 97
Ellis Sports Ground 109
Ellis, Joseph 23, 47, 71
Ellis, Joseph Valentine 74, 75
Ennerdale Hall 30
Europe 7

125

Fabrication shop 81
Ferro-alloys 77
Ferro-manganese 23, 24, 83
Finishing mill 102
Finishing strand 102
Firebrick 96, 107
Fireclay 106, 107
First World War 74, 75, 76, 77, 79
Fisher Street 70
Fishplate mill 47
Fishplate(s) 103
Fletcher, Issac 27
Foundry 7, 81, 121
France 74
Frazer, Mr 27
Frizington 29, 68
Furness Railway (FR) 76

Ganister 96
Gas 109
Gas holder 109
Gasworks 15
General Strike 75
George, Lloyd 75
Germany 21, 71
Gibson, Mary 41
Goodmans 81
Government control 112
Graham, Thomas Whitely 74, 75, 79
Griffiths, William Ivander 15

Ha'penny Billy's bridge 36
Haematite mines 68
Harbour 23, 56, 58
Harmer, W.T.V 79
Harrington 13, 40, 41, 56, 58, 70, 109
Harrington Iron & Coal Co. 23, 71
Harrington Road 43, 75
Henderson & Davis 15
Heslop Steam Engine 13, 14
Heslop, Adam 13, 14, 15
Heslop, Crosby 15
Heslop, Millward & Co. 13
Heslop, Milward, Johnson & Co. 15
Heslop, Thomas 15
Hicks, William 11
Highton, Edward 46
Highton, Robert Ernest 46, 47, 71
Hodgson, Richard Harrison 67
Hoey, David George 35
Holegill 11
Holley bottom(s) 107
Hopper wagon(s) 108
Hot metal mixer 86, 87, 88
How Michael 57
Huntrods, Joseph 59
Hydraulic power 51

India 43, 67, 68
Ingot moulds 62, 96, 97, 100
Ingot(s) 52, 96
Iron & Steel Institute 29, 59
Iron castings 81

Iron ore 7, 15, 21, 30, 32, 68, 108
Italy 21

Jamieson, Hugh 35
Jane Pit 56
Japan 68
Jars, Gabriel 11
John Street 75

Kenyon, Henry 41
Keswick 46
Kilmarnock 63
King George V 74, 75
Kirk Bros. 59
Kirk family 57, 59
Kirk, Henry 59
Kirk, Mary Ann 41, 45
Kirk, Peter 23, 41, 42, 43, 45, 46
Kirkland (USA) 45

Labour Party 43
Laird Brothers Ltd. 68
Lake Washington 45
Ledger, Joseph 23, 43
Ley, James Peard 15
Limestone 31
Linefoot 43
Locomotive(s) 108
Loewy 117
Loewy Press 117
London North Western Railway (LNWR) 18, 37, 40, 58, 65
Lonsdale Dock 18, 19, 34, 35, 37, 68
Lonsdale Park 76
Lonsdale, Lord 75
Low Station 36, 38, 56, 57, 58, 65, 75
Low Wreah pit 14
Lowca 13, 15
Lowca Ironworks 15
Lowther Haematite Iron & Steel Co. 33, 36
Lowther Haematite Iron Co. 33, 35
Lowther Ironworks 7, 30, 34, 36, 37, 38
Lowther family 11

Machine shop 81, 121
Mallalieu, F 47
Manchester 29
Manganese 71
Marsh & Quay 59
Marshside 59
Marshside Ironworks 55, 57, 59
Maryport 18, 19, 27, 36, 37, 38, 59
Merchants Quay 34
Micklam Brickworks 106
Mild steel 79
Miller & Anderson 41
Millfield 10
Mining equipment 81
Ministry of Munitions 75
Ministry of Supply 79
Mixer, hot metal 86, 87, 88
Moorbank colliery 56

Mordy, John 12
Morrison, Mr 59
Moss Bay 7, 15, 20, 40, 41, 43, 45, 46, 47, 50, 63, 65, 67, 70, 74, 77, 79, 81, 83, 84, 88, 96, 100, 102, 103, 104, 105, 116, 117
Moss Bay Bessemer Training School 20
Moss Bay Haematite Iron & Steel Co. 23, 42, 43, 45, 46, 47, 71, 76
Moss Bay Haematite Iron Co. 7, 39, 41, 42, 43
Moss Bay Ironworks 44, 46, 83
Moss Bay Steel plant 50, 51, 105
Moulding sheds 58
Munitions 74, 75, 76, 79
Murray, David 81
Mysore, India 71

Napthalene 109
National Coal Board 120
National Gas Board 109
Nationalisation 79, 83, 120
New South Wales 68
New Yard 56, 58, 63
New Yard Ironworks 7, 55, 56, 57, 58, 59, 65, 70
North Africa 68
North America 7
North Eastern Railway 68
North Western Iron & Steel Co. 25, 32
North of England Haematite Iron Co 7, 33, 35
Northside 37

Oates family 68
Old company 21
Oldside 15, 18, 19, 20, 21, 23, 24, 27, 34, 36, 37, 70
Oldside Iron & Steel Works 17, 23, 24, 36, 37
Open hearth furnace 47, 68
Owens College 29
Oxford Street 75
Oxygen lance 82

Paris Exhibition 31
Paterson, Mr 79
Pig beds 30, 74, 75, 77
Pig casting 78
Pig casting 110-113
Pig iron 7, 11, 19, 20, 21, 23, 26, 27, 28, 29, 30, 32, 41, 46, 47, 50, 59, 63, 66, 75, 77, 78, 80, 86, 88, 110
Pig iron moulds 110, 112, 113
Ponsonby, John 11
Price & Dixon 59
Prince of Wales Dock 23, 34
Puddling 29
Puddling furnace(s) 27, 57, 58, 59
Puget Sound Construction Co. 45
Purser, Josiah 67

Quayside Forge 41, 57
Quayside Ironworks 15, 41
Queen Mary 74, 75
Quirk, Peter Gibson 23, 43

Rail bank 116
Rail finishing 81, 116
Rail mill 71, 81
Railway lines see Steel rails
Railway sleepers 43, 62, 117
Railway wagons, 112
Railways 8
Randles, John Scurrah 23, 46, 47, 71, 74, 75, 76
Recession 32, 77
Regenerative hot-blast stove 83
River Derwent 7, 10, 11, 13, 16, 18, 19, 27, 34, 35, 36, 79, 105, 123
Roberts, Charles (of Wakefield) 108
Rolling mill(s) 41, 52, 59, 83, 100, 101, 102
Roscoe, Professor 29
Rotherham 77
Roughing mill 102
Royal School of Mines 29
Royal Train 75

Samuel Fox 77
San Juan Islands 42
Schofield, Richard 42
Science Museum 14
Scotland 11
Seaton Ironworks 7, 8, 11, 12, 13, 14, 15, 16, 34
Seattle 45, 46
Second World War 77, 79, 81, 120
Shaker conveyors 81
Sheffield 21, 63, 67, 68, 77
Shell steel 75, 76
Shipbuilding 8, 12, 13, 21
Shore works 79
Siddick 18, 32, 37
Sinter 120
Sinter plant 120
Skiddies 19, 20, 23, 27
Skyrin, William 11
Slag 80, 104, 105
Slag bank(s) 105
Smith, Joseph 19, 21
Smith, Samual Wagstaffe 15
Snelus, George James 26, 28, 29, 31
Soaking pits 49, 52, 100
Solway Colliery 70, 109, 120
Solway Firth 12, 105
South Gut 34
Spain 68

Spedding, Dickinson, Russell & Co. 13
Spedding, Hicks & Co. 11, 13
Spedding, Hicks, Senhouse & Co. 13
Spedding, James 11
Spedding, Thomas 11
Spiegel 23, 24, 83, 93
Spoil heaps see Slag bank
St Michaels Church 15
St Michaels Road 43
Staffordshire 21
Stainburn 10, 13, 76
Stainless steel 79
Stanley Street 15, 41, 57, 59
Station Road 75
Steam power 13, 14, 19, 20, 57
Steel 23, 30, 36
Steel bloom(s) 100, 101
Steel making 21, 22, 26, 28, 29, 40, 41, 46, 47, 48, 50, 52, 54, 62, 63, 74, 75, 86-96, 105
Steel plate 117
Steel prices 31
Steel rails 30, 29, 41, 45, 52, 62, 68, 77, 81, 103
Steel sleepers see Railway sleepers
Steel, Peech and Tozer 77
Steel, heat treated 79
Stein, Alan J. 45
Stephenson, George 57
Stephenson, Robert 108
Stewart Demag 88, 92
Stilecroft House 76
Stocksbridge 77
Stoves 13
Stripper crane 49, 96, 100
Sugden, Edward Haigh 11, 29

Tacoma 45
Teeming 51, 52, 54, 95, 97
Teeming ladle(s) 96, 97
Telford, Messrs 27
Thomas, Sydney 29
Thompson, Joseph 67
Thorburn, Mr. 19
Tin bar 68
Tinplate 15
Tomlinson, William 67
Trade Union movement 43
Transfer crane 49
Tulk, John Augustus 15
Tulk, Ley & Co. 15
Tunnellers 81
Tuyere bottom(s) 107
Tuyere(s) 31, 88, 92, 106, 107
Tyre mill 71

Unemployment 77
United States 71
United Steel Companies 8, 66, 69, 77, 79, 80, 82, 83, 86, 106, 109, 110, 120, 121
United Steel Group 77

Valentine, Charles James 23, 41, 42, 43, 46, 71
Valentine, Herbert 23, 47, 71
Vancover 46
Vulcan 70

Waggonway 56
Wagon(s), hopper 108
Wagon(s), railway 54, 112
Walls, Catherine 43
Walls, Patrick 43, 71, 75
Water power 10, 16
Watt, James 14
Watters, Robert 11
Wattleworth, Douglas R. 41, 57
Wellman 86, 96
West Cumberland Haematite Iron Co. 7, 18, 25, 27
West Cumberland Iron & Steel Co. 25, 26, 29, 30, 31, 32, 35, 37, 43
Westfield 7, 67
Whitehaven 13, 14, 44
Whitehaven Junction Railway (WJR) 18, 19, 27, 35, 37, 40, 54, 56, 57, 58, 65
Williams, H. B. 75
Wilson Cammell & Co. 63, 67
Wilson family 67, 68
Wilson, H. E. 71
Wilson, William 35
Woodhall, Ducklam & Co. 77, 109
Workington Bridge 11
Workington Bridge & Boiler Co. 57
Workington Haematite Iron & Steel Co. 17, 23, 24, 29
Workington Haematite Iron Co. 7, 17, 18, 19, 20, 21, 27, 30, 31, 37
Workington Iron & Steel Co. 8, 23, 24, 44, 47, 59, 62, 68, 69, 70, 71, 72, 73, 74, 76, 77, 79, 83, 105, 108, 116, 120
Workington Iron Co. 17, 23, 36
Workington Munition Girls' Football team 76
Workington, Borough of 70, 76
Wrought iron 11, 41

Yeathouse 15
Yorkshire 63

Other local interest titles published by Tempus:

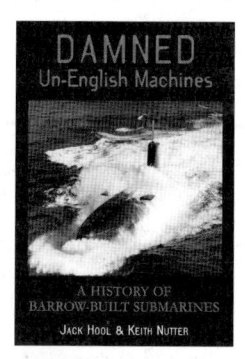

Damned Un-English Machines A History of Barrow-Built Submarines
JACK HOOL AND KEITH NUTTER

The shipbuilding works at Barrow-in-Furness have been the hub of the Royal Navy's submarine-building programme for more than a century. This comprehensive treatment of the subject, including references to commercial 'mini-subs', First and Second World War German submarines and the reactivation of the Canadian Upholder Class, provides an exceptional narrative that will become a valuable reference in the future.
0 7524 2781 4

Workington Association Football Club
PAUL EADE

From the early days in the North Eastern League, this book of over 200 images charts Workington's entry into the Football League in 1951, the 26 years spent there, and the Reds' fortunes since their return to non-League football in 1977. Particular tribute is paid to the Football League period, including Bill Shankly's period as Workington manager from 1954 to 1955 and the classic FA Cup tie at Borough Park in January 1958 when the Reds hosted Manchester United in front of a record 21,000-strong crowd.
0 7524 2818 7

Whitehaven History & Guide
ALAN W. ROUTLEDGE

This history of Whitehaven tells the story of the town from the time of its first Roman fort to the present day. Mining was once so intensive here that 3,800 workers raised 232 tons of coal per man per year, and the harbour was at one time the most important in the country after London. As well as an in-depth history of the area, its people and its industrial past, this book explores the various local landmarks of Whitehaven, and also includes a guided tour which enables the reader to embark on a tour of the fascinating harbour area, to explore the Beacon, the Quays and the Marina.
0 7524 2602 8

Carlisle Remembered
DENIS PERRIAM

The memories collected here are from letters written in response to Mary Burgess's column that featured in the *Cumberland News* between 1955 and 1978; with minimal editing, a variety of extracts from those letters have been selected to cover as many facets of Carlisle's recent history as possible. Some of the early correspondents, born in the 1870s, remember hangings in the gaol, Jimmy Dyer playing his fiddle and troops marching off to the Boer War. Later correspondents share memories of the first aircraft, Empire Day, holidays at the seaside and listening to the wireless.
0 7524 1678 2

To discover more Tempus titles please visit us at:
www.tempus-publishing.com